MW00526621

MEL BAY PRESENTS

FRETBOARD BASICS

BY ARNIE BERLE

FOREWORD

I am a very lucky man. I'm lucky because I've been successful in so many different areas of the music business. I've had the fun and excitement that goes with playing and travelling with what used to be known as the "name bands." I've enjoyed great success as the busiest private music teacher in the New York and Westchester County area. I've had the thrill of seeing some of the many books I've had published, in stores all across the country. Since 1977 I've had the honor and prestige that comes with being a professor of music at Mercy College, a very fine college located in Dobbs Ferry, New York. But the biggest kick and the greatest satisfaction and sense of fulfillment has come from the many letters I've received from all over the world in response to my "Fretboard Basics" columns in *Guitar Player Magazine*.

Nothing could be more gratifying for a teacher than to receive letters that say "you have a way of cutting through all the baloney and getting right down to the nitty-gritty" or, "I've played and studied guitar for so many years but it was your columns that helped me understand things that have confused me for years." That's the common link that runs through so many of my letters, that I have helped clear away some confusion for so many people.

This book could not have been done without the help of some people who I want to thank. I would like to thank Miller Freeman Publications for giving me permission to use this collection of my columns, and Bill Bay of Mel Bay Publications, Inc. for encouraging me to put these columns into a book for publication. Bill has published two other books of mine, *How To Create and Develop a Jazz Solo* and *Jazz Licks, Phrases and Patterns*. Throughout all these projects Bill has been a gentleman to work with and has allowed me full creative freedom without any restraints.

To my wife Rosalie I want to dedicate this book. She has been the motivating force behind all of my successes. Thanks for keeping my suppers warm all these years.

I want to thank all those readers of *Guitar Player Magazine* who took the time to write all those letters. I'm sorry I didn't get a chance to answer all of them. I hope some of these columns bring back memories. To the new readers of these columns, I hope something here will help to demystify something for you. Lastly, to everybody I want to say, till next time, remember, "straight ahead."

Arnie Berle

ARNIE BERLE BIO

Arnie began his professional career in the early 1950s and quickly became a member of one of the leading dance bands in the country, Johnny Long. He played saxophone and clarinet, and was flute soloist with the band. They travelled all over the country playing theatres and nightclubs. After leaving Johnny Long, Arnie worked with a number of other big bands but he decided that being a road musician was not for him.

Settling back in his home town of New York, Arnie soon became very active as a free-lance musician gaining experience doing shows, Latin work, jazz bands and a great variety of work as a club date player.

His vast musical experience attracted other musicians to want to study with him and he soon found himself in much demand as a teacher. Arnie found out that he loved teaching and before long he built up the largest private teaching practice in the New York and Westchester County area.

In 1964 with the arrival of the Beatles and the subsequent "British Invasion," Arnie decided to study the guitar. He went through a long period of study with the very best teachers and players in New York. His previous musical experiences gave him a view of the guitar that was much broader than that of most guitar players who play just one instrument. In addition to the guitar, Arnie had already studied the accordion and the vibraphone with the best players in the country. As a matter of fact, in 1957 Arnie had written the first accordion instruction book to be accompanied by a recording, and in 1968 he had written for another publisher the most unique book for mallet instruments.

In 1975 Arnie began writing for *Guitar Player Magazine* starting out with interviews of the leading guitarists in the country and then doing feature articles. In 1978 he began his very popular column, "Fretboard Basics." At this time Arnie had already earned his BA degree in music and was teaching music at Mercy College in Dobbs Ferry, New York.

Today Arnie is a full time professor at Mercy College and still teaches privately at his home in Yonkers, New York. He has been included in the *International Who's Who in Music* and continues to write instructional books.

Arnie Berle's
FRETBOARD BASICS

APRIL 1978

The Modes And Related Chords

Arnie Berle has written numerous interviews and articles in Guitar Player, covering a variety of musical subjects, including jazz chords [see GP, Oct. '77]. His most recent article was "The Harmonized Scale" [see GP, Mar. '78], in which he described the process of building chords from scales. He is well-known for his performing and teaching, as well as his writing—he is the author of nearly two dozen books on guitar playing, including "Modern Chords And Progressions For Guitar "(Amsco Music Publishing 33 W. 60th St. New York NY 10023). A graduate Of New York's Empire State College, Arnie has one of the largest private teaching practices on the East Coast (87 Candlewood Dr., Yonkers, NY 10710).

I'D LIKE TO TALK ABOUT A SUBJECT THAT EVERY GUITAR player must surely be familiar with, but one that I look at just a little differently. As a student I recall being taught that chords are formed by taking the 1st, 3rd, and 5th notes of the major scale. That's fine; I still teach that to some of my students. Then, of course, to form the minor chord, you simply lower the 3rd of the major chord one half-step. Another way to teach the construction of chords is through the building of thirds: e.g., adding a minor third over a major third produces a major chord, and by adding a major third over a minor third, we get a minor chord. Then we can add a major third to a major chord and have a major 7th chord. Adding a minor third over a major chord gives us a dominant 7th. The examples below illustrate this.

All of the above is correct, and chords should be understood in terms of thirds being built on top of other thirds.

Another way that the structure of chords is taught is by writing out a scale and telling the student to build chords over each note of the scale ascending in thirds, or by adding a note on every line or space above the scale note. For example, if the scale note is written on a line, then place notes on the next two lines above. If the scale note is in a space, then, add notes on the next two spaces above (see the example below):

Again, the end result is correct. You will arrive at the diatonic (meaning that the chords contain only notes from that scale) series of chords for that scale. Now I would like to demonstrate another way of teaching chords that I believe will have more meaning, especially for the student who intends to go into improvisation. First, I write out the major scale. Then, as my first teacher told me, I take the 1st, 3rd, 5th, and 7th notes (my first teacher didn't mention the 7th note, but I do), and I form my chord. In the example below, I have used this process to produce a *Cmaj7* chord:

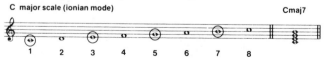

Now, I write out the same scale, (C), but this time, I start from the second note (D), and I write the scale up to the D, an octave higher. What we now have is a new kind of scale called a mode. This one is called the dorian mode.

In this case, it's the *D* dorian mode because it begins on the *D* note. Taking the 1st, 3rd, 5th, and 7th notes from this mode I have the *Dm7* chord:

Next, I again write out the *C* scale, but this time, we're starting from the third note (*E*). Now we have another scale called the phrygian mode. Taking the 1st, 3rd, 5th, and 7th notes from this mode I have the *Em7* chord:

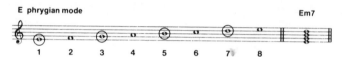

I continue the same process through all the rest of the notes on the C scale and I create new modes. Then I create new chords by taking the 1st, 3rd, 5th, and 7th notes from each of these modes. Here they are written out:

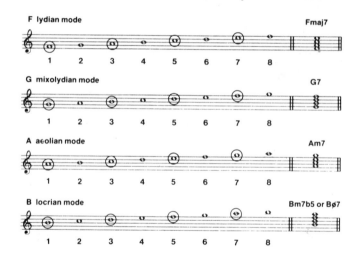

At this point, having shown how all the chords are formed from the various modes within the major scale, I place each chord over its respective starting note of the original scale (in this case it's the *C* scale). Here are the diatonic chords built from each note of the *C* major scale:

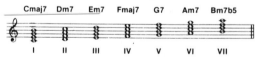

Notice that the chords are numbered with Roman numerals, according to their position within the major scale.

For added practice, the student should write out several major scales and then write out the modes derived from each scale, as well as the chords derived from each mode. In my teaching of chords, this is the method I use, because I believe it gives the student a better understanding of chords in relation to a particular key, rather than just as an isolated combination of notes. It is also good preparation for the study of improvisation, since the modes become the improvising scales for each particular chord.

I would like to hear from any students and teachers who have any problems concerning the concepts I cover, as well as from those who have suggestions for my column. You can write to me in care of *Guitar Player*. Thanks!

Tonal Center—Key Area

TONAL CENTER, KEY AREA, KEY FEELING—THESE ARE all phrases that have become common in articles and books on jazz improvisation. I'd like to discuss the meaning and the importance of these phrases to the guitarist, as an accompanist and as an improviser.

The whole foundation of our harmonic system depends on the concept of key or tonality. A definition of a key that I give to my students is that it is "a group of related pitches." The simplest way of demonstrating this is to play a little tune first in one key and then in another. The distance from one note (or pitch) to another remains the same from one key to the next; the only thing that changes is the level of pitch—it's either higher or lower. This ability to transpose music from one level of pitch to another, without changing the relationships of the notes, is the basis for both the system of harmony and the concept of key or tonality. Within any given key, one note always acts as a point of rest, a stationary center toward which all the other notes move. This note or point of rest is called the keynote or tonic.

When the notes or pitches of a particular key are placed in a pre-established order (whole-step, whole-step, half-step, etc.), we have a scale, and the keynote or tonic becomes the first note. In the March '78 issue of GP [see The Harmonized Scale], I showed how chords are formed from the notes of the scale. (Within each major scale there are six additional scales called *modes*. Taking the 1st, 3rd, 5th, and 7th notes of the major scale and each of the modes, we form the diatonic series of chords, which are used to harmonize any melodies based on that key.)

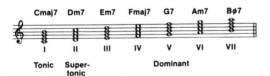

The chord built on the tonic note is called the tonic chord, or to use the more common terminology, the I chord. This I chord then becomes the center to which all the other chords gravitate; it is the point of rest in any conventional progression—the point of ending. Key or tonality depends on a sense of stability—to be in a key means that a composition must begin and end in that key and must center around it. The key must be established by the use of its primary chords.

If the I chord is a chord of rest or stability, then a chord that is the complete opposite is the *dominant*, or the V chord. This is a chord of unrest, a chord of movement; it demands resolution, and it wants to move to the I chord. For example, play a *G7* chord and listen very carefully to it sort of "hanging." It gives the feeling of unrest, of wanting to go someplace. Now play the *C* chord. Hear the feeling of rest, or resolution, a sense of motion resolving to a point of rest. To carry this one step further: In the same way that the V chord wants to go to the I, this principle can be extended by finding a chord that wants to move to the V. That chord is the *supertonic*, or the II chord.

These three chords are known as the primary chords and are used to establish a key feeling, a tonal center, a key area.

When you realize that in any musical composition there could be any number of key changes before the tune actually ends, you understand why it's so important for the guitarist to recognize these key changes or tonal centers by picking out the II-V-I chords of each new key. Many times, a composer will just have a series of II-V chords going through several tonal centers before finally reaching the I chord at the end of the composition. Again, the guitarist must recognize these key changes and have a number of different ways in which to play these chords in every key. For the improvising musician, it's even more important to recognize these key changes in order to know which scales to play over the changing tonal centers. Below is a chart showing the II-V-I chords in every major key. These should be memorized:

Key	II	V	I
C	Dm7	G7	Cmaj7
F	Gm7	C7	Fmaj7
B♭	Cm7	F7	B♭maj7
E♭	Fm7	B♭7	E♭maj7
A♭	B♭m7	E♭7	A♭maj7
D♭	E♭m7	A♭7	D♭maj7
G♭	A♭m7	D♭7	G♭maj7
B	C♯m7	F♯7	Bmaj7
E	F♯m7	B7	Emaj7
A	Bm7	E7	Amaj7
D	Em7	A7	Dmaj7
G	Am7	D7	Gmaj7

Now let's take a standard tune used by all jazz players and see how the various tonal centers or key areas are indicated by the use of the II-V chords. The tune is "Satin Doll," written by Duke Ellington. All the tonal centers are bracketed. Notice in the sixth measure the use of the A♭m7-D♭7 going to the Cmaj7 (the I chord in this key). These chords were used to harmonize the original melody of that measure and may be considered a substitutional device to avoid the usual V to I motion. I will discuss these substitutions in future columns.

Any questions and comments or suggestions for future topics will be greatly appreciated. Send them to me c/o *Guitar Player.*

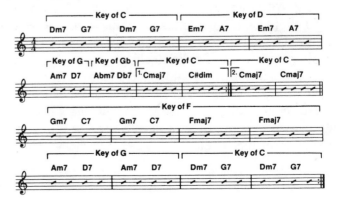

Arnie Berle's
FRETBOARD BASICS

June 1978

Those "Other" Chords

MUCH HAS BEEN WRITTEN ABOUT THE II, V, and I chords and the importance of being able to recognize them in tunes as temporary modulations into new tonal centers or key areas [see my column for May '78]. I thought I would take a little time this month and talk about those "other" chords—the III, IV, VI, and VII chords. Let's look at the diatonic series of chords once again as a point of reference:

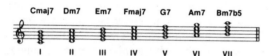

The VII chord. To begin with, it's important to understand that all of the seventh chords shown above can be extended to ninth chords. With that in mind, if we extend the V chord *(G7,* in the key of *C)* to a ninth *(G9),* and compare the VII chord *(Bm7♭5)* to the *G9,* we find four common tones (see below). Therefore, because of these common tones, the VII chord may be considered as a substitute for the V chord.

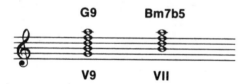

The VI chord. I have to explain something before we talk about the VI: In popular or jazz harmony, the I (which you see above as a major 7th chord) is quite often made into a maj6th chord. That is, the 1st, 3rd, 5th, and 6th notes of the major scale give you a 6th chord, so that the *Cmaj7* could very easily be a *C6.* Quite often, the two are used together *(Cmaj7-C6).* Now, if we think of the I chord above as a 6th chord *(C6),* and look at the notes of the VI chord *(Am7),* we find exactly the same notes (see below). Therefore, many theorists believe that the VI chord is a substitute for the I6 chord. Also, usage very often dictates the rule, and many songs contain the progression of I-VI-II-V. For example, "Heart And Soul," "These Foolish Things," "Blue Moon," "Ringo's Theme," and many others use this formula. So, we will treat the movement of the VI chord as we would the V. The V usually moves to I, so—keeping the same relationship—the VI will progress to II. For a good example of this motion, check out "All The Things You Are."

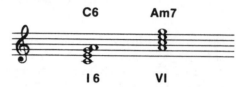

The IV chord. Just as we extended the *G7* chord to a *G9,* let's extend the II chord *(Dm7)* to a 9th chord *(Dm9).* Comparing the IV chord *(Fmaj7)* to the IIm9 *(Dm9),* we find four common tones (see below). Therefore, the IV chord may be considered as a substitute chord for the II. The II chord is the preferred chord when the next chord is a V, as in the case of the II-V progression. Many tunes based on simple harmonic structures, such as folk music or blues, still use the IV chord. Remember that the IV chord, like the I, is often a major 7th and offers a feeling of rest, rather than movement. It is sometimes treated as a temporary I (as in the blues).

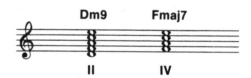

The III chord. If we extend the I chord *(Cmaj7)* to the 9th *(Cmaj9),* and compare the notes of the Imaj9 to the IIIm7 *(Em7),* again, we find four common tones (see below). The III chord is therefore used as a substitute for the I chord.

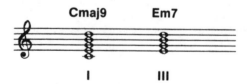

I'm sure a few of you music majors will have some comments to make on things I've said above; I would certainly welcome them. Let's hear from you.

Those "Other" Chords

IN THE MARCH '78 ISSUE OF *GUITAR PLAYER,* I DID AN ARTICLE called The Harmonized Scale, and the number of letters I have received from readers expressing their interest and desire for more information on the subject is the reason for continuing the discussion in this column. Playing harmonized scales, no doubt, is the best way of learning to play chords all over the fingerboard in a very organized and systematic way. Let's begin by reviewing what we did in the original article. First we have to divide the fingerboard into three overlapping sets of four strings each:

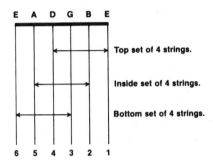

Now we're going to play a series of chords on each set of strings. The first group of chords is to be played on the bottom set of four strings.

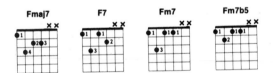

Notice that the root of each chord is played on the sixth string. Play each of the chord types up the fingerboard chromatically, and be sure to memorize the name of each chord at every fret. Below is an abbreviated example that shows the chords at each fret along the sixth string.

Let's move on to the chords played on the inside set of four strings; this time the root of each chord is played on the fifth string:

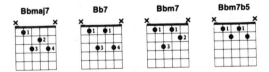

Once again, play the above chords up the fingerboard chromatically. Play each type and memorize the name of each one at all frets. Below is an abbreviated example that shows the chords at each fret along the fifth string.

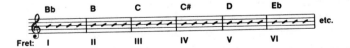

Here are the chords played on the top set of four strings; the root of each chord will be played on the fourth string:

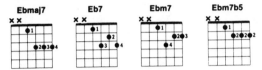

Below is an abbreviated example that shows the chords at each fret along the fourth string. Play each of the above chords up the fingerboard and memorize the names of the chords in each position. Follow this pattern:

By using combinations of the three sets of chords we have covered, it is possible to realize all of the harmonized scales. Below are four exercises that combine what we have learned so far. The circled numbers indicate on which string to play the root of the chord.

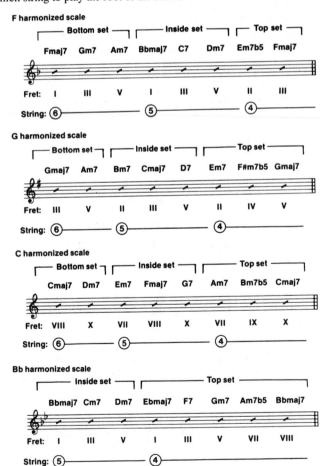

Notice that the *C* scale could have been started on the 3rd fret using the inside set of strings, and the *Bb* scale could have been started on the sixth fret using the bottom set of strings. Try playing other scales using different combinations of strings. Next month I'll show how to use these chords in some progressions and in studies with the circle of fifths.

Arnie Berle's
FRETBOARD BASICS

The Harmonized Scale, Part II

IN THE JULY '78 ISSUE OF *GP* WE REVIEWED THE HARMO-nized scales, which can be employed by using combinations of chord forms played over three sets of four adjacent strings each. In my teaching I very often find that some students will learn a new chord form from one of those books that illustrates 10,000 chords, but they never realize that the chord isn't really learned until it can be played all over the fingerboard and then fit into a progression. So this month I'd like to have you play all the chords shown last month *all over the fingerboard.* Then we'll try them in some very common progressions.

First of all, let's work on the chords on the bottom set of four strings. For all of you new readers, here are the chord forms used last month:

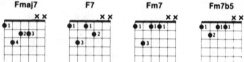

The following exercise is based on the cycle of fifths. Only the letter-name of each chord is given. Play the exercise first using all major 7th chords, then play it again, this time using dominant 7th chords. Continue playing the exercise using the minor 7ths and then again with the minor 7♭5 chords. Incidentally, the minor 7♭5 is also called a *half-diminished* chord.

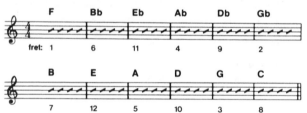

Here are last month's chords played on the inside set of four strings:

The following example is again based on the cycle of fifths. Play the exercise four times, again using the four different types of chords. Notice that this time I'm starting the cycle from *B♭.* The cycle may be started from any chord.

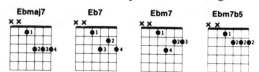

Here are the chords on the top set of four strings:

Again the exercise is based on the cycle of fifths, and this time I start from *E♭.* Play this four times using each of the above chord qualities:

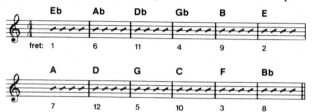

Now that you can play all of these chords in several positions, let's see how it's possible to play through the cycle without unnecessary jumping all over the board. Below are several ways of working through the cycle of fifths by using combinations of the three sets of four strings. In each exercise the number in the circle indicates the string on which the lowest note is played. Play each example using all of these chord qualities: major 7th, dominant 7th, minor 7th, and minor 7♭5.

Exercise 1.

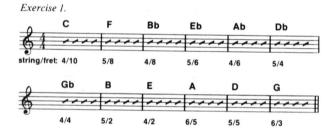

Exercise 2.

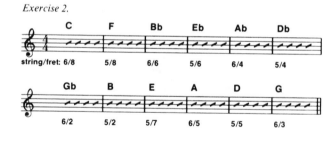

Exercise 3.

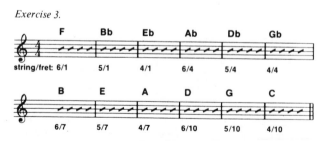

The above exercises should give you a good knowledge of the fingerboard. Take your time and go through them slowly. Try to make up some exercises on your own, remembering that the whole purpose is to get to know the fingerboard. Don't just limit yourself to learning a new chord form in one position. Next month we'll put these chords into some of the more commonly used progressions.

8

Arnie Berle's
FRETBOARD BASICS

Two Common Chord Progressions

IN THE JULY AND AUGUST COLUMNS WE LEARNED HOW to play chords on the bottom set of four strings (*G, D, A, E*), on the inside set of four strings (*B, G, D, A*), and on the top set of four strings (*E, B, G, D*). The chords were the major 7th, dominant 7th, minor 7th, and minor 7♭5th. You played the chords chromatically up the fingerboard and around the cycle. Now we are going to use the chords in context; in other words we are going to use them in common progressions, just as you might find them in an actual playing situation.

The most common progression in the jazz and popular music idioms is the IIm-V-I sequence. Although I have written about this before (in the May '78 column), the importance of being able to play this progression in as many ways as you can—all over the fingerboard cannot be overemphasized. An examination of any batch of tunes played by jazz artists since the 1930s up to the present will illustrate the extensive applications of the IIm-V-I. Another progression found in so many standard tunes, and which was used a great deal by writers in the early days of rock and roll, is the I-VIm-IIm-V progression. A brief list of tunes which contain the two progressions is given at the end of this column. Now let's see some of the ways in which these may be played using the chords that you learned from the last two columns. Below are several ways in which to play a IIm-V-I progression (the first three examples are very useful when comping rhythm).

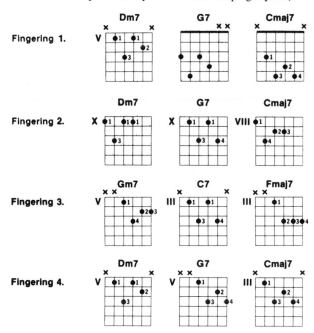

Another very common fingering for the IIm-V-I progression is shown below. Notice that the chords originally played on the bottom set of four strings are now played in more open voicings. The note played on the fifth (*A*) string is now played on the second (*B*) string, one octave higher. Notice also the new fingering for the dominant 7th chord. Play the progression up the fingerboard.

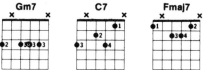

The following are the IIm-V-I chords in every major key. Play through the entire exercise using the various fingerings shown above. The choices are yours.

Here are two fingerings for the I-VIm-IIm-V progression.

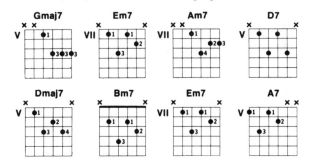

The following are the I-VIm-IIm-V chords in every major key. Using either of the two sets of fingerings shown above, play through the entire exercise.

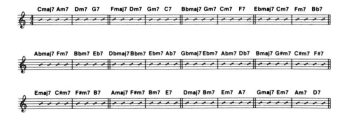

Naturally there are many, many more ways to play the two progressions just given, and we will cover these other ways in future columns. The fingerings you have just learned are very basic and did not make use of common tones which would have made smoother movement from chord to chord. (Common tones will be covered in future columns.) Below is a listing of some popular and jazz standards which contain the IIm-V-I progression, and others that contain the I-VIm-IIm-V sequence. Songs with the IIm-V-I sequence include: "Laura," "I'm In The Mood For Love," "Don't Blame Me," "Little Green Apples," "Autumn Leaves," "By The Time I Get To Phoenix," "How High The Moon," "Giant Steps," and "Pick Yourself Up." Some of the songs with the I-VIm-IIm-V sequence are: "Heart And Soul," "Blue Moon," "Earth Angel," "Put Your Head On My Shoulder," "Ringo's Theme (This Boy)," "I Love How You Love Me," "I Got Rhythm," and "Dizzy Atmosphere."

Both lists of songs could go on and on; however, space limits other inclusions. In future columns we will cover more ways in which these progressions can be played, both chordally and melodically.

Arnie Berle's
FRETBOARD BASICS

October 1978

Improvisation, Scales, And Modes

SOME TIME AGO I HAD A BOOK PUBLISHED BY MUSIC SALES Corp. (33 West 60th St., New York, NY 10023), called *The Complete Handbook For Jazz Improvisation* (the title was chosen by the publisher). At its conclusion I stated that the study of jazz improvisation is never truly completed. The jazz musician is constantly searching for new techniques and fresh ideas; it's a lifetime endeavor. Recently I was having dinner with two leading jazz musicians, and one of them started talking about all the books I had published and all the teaching that I do. I said to him that I would gladly exchange all of it for just one chorus of an improvised solo of mine that would cause somebody in the audience to say "yeah!" This player, who is so great and whom I admire so much, said to me, "Never mind one chorus, we're all trying to play just *eight bars* to get that 'yeah.'" The point, of course, is that the great players whom we admire so much are skilled technicians who are constantly in search of that rare moment when everything seems to come together and the result seems divinely inspired. Of course some players seem to be able to get it together more often than others, and they become the influences that others emulate.

This is not meant to discourage anyone, but rather to put the task of learning to improvise into the proper perspective. As my good friend Gene Bertoncini said in his interview in *GP* [Oct. '77]: "You have to develop the two areas that go into making up a musician, the intellectual and the intuitive. The intellectual is developed by working on the knowledge of the fingerboard through scales of all kinds, played vertically and horizontally." He goes on to say that you "fill your computer till this is all down in your subconscious, ready to be called upon. The intuitive side, which can also be studied and practiced, involves developing a good sense of time, listening to all kinds of music, and in general, responding in a sensitive way to the human beings around you."

So, now you have it. You must practice, and you must expose yourself to the kind of music you want to play; in fact, you should listen to all kinds of music and to players of all instruments. Listening is a very important part in the development of a good improviser.

Now for the task at hand. We shall begin at the most fundamental step in learning to improvise the ability to play scales of all kinds all over the fingerboard. The guitar is unique in that it allows you to play any scale with several fingerings and in many locations on the fingerboard. On instruments such as the saxophone, clarinet, and

flute, a *C* major scale beginning at *C* below the staff can only be fingered one way, but on the guitar it may be fingered a number of different ways. It is this multiplicity of fingerings which seems to cause the greatest confusion for the guitar student. On the other hand, there is one advantage that the guitarist has that most other instrumentalists do not have—the ease in moving from key to key without changing the fingering. Just as chords are movable, so are scales.

Let's begin by learning our first scale fingering. In my own private teaching I find it better to give one fingering at a time in order to avoid confusion. The diagram below illustrates the fingering for the *G* major scale, with the tonic note *G* played on the sixth string at the 3rd fret. Notice that it is possible to extend the scale to one note below the lowest tonic and one note above the highest tonic without changing positions.

The musical notation for the *G* scale is shown below:

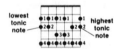

After you are thoroughly familiar with the fingering, play the pattern starting from the 2nd fret, which produces the *Gb* scale. Next, play scales from each fret along the sixth string. The following table shows the name of the scale played at each fret:

Fret:	2	3	4	5	6	7	8	9	10	11	12	13
Scale:	Gb F#	G	Ab	A	Bb	B	C	Db C#	D	Eb	E	F

Since improvisation is basically the creating of melodies based on a particular series of scales or chords, it is important that you begin to build a melodic vocabulary to be used as a foundation for creating your melodic ideas. The following exercises shown in the key of *G* should be practiced in all keys up the fingerboard. (All fingerings are given for those who do not read musical notation.) Next month we will continue with the subjects of scales and modes and their uses in improvisation.

Ex. 1.

Ex. 2.

Ex. 3.

Ex. 4.

Improvisation, Scales, And Modes, Part II

LAST MONTH WE LEARNED A FINGERING FOR THE *G* scale, starting from the 3rd fret on the sixth string. Since we will be learning a lot of different scale fingerings in future columns, we must have a way of distinguishing one fingering from another, so I'll arbitrarily call this first fingering "Form 1." At this point, using the Form I fingering starting at the 2nd fret on the sixth string, you should be able to play from the *G♭* scale up to the *E* scale at the 12th fret (and even higher if you have a cutaway guitar).

Now, rather than giving you all the other scale fingerings at this time, as some books and columns do, I would rather concentrate on this one scale fingering so that you can better understand terms such as "modes," "chord scales," "improvisation," "patterns," etc. According to all the mail I get, these words seem to cause the greatest amount of confusion, so instead of throwing a batch of scale fingerings at you and then showing how to connect all the scales, I'd rather take it bit by bit in small doses. It will take some time and practice to gain proficiency with scales. As a matter of fact—just to digress for a minute—in the April '78 issue of *GP* I did an interview with Herb Ellis in which he said, "If you put a gun to my head and asked me to play a three-octave scale, I couldn't do it." What he meant was that playing a three-octave scale in itself doesn't make you a jazz player. One more thing: At this point it would be helpful to review my column on "The Modes And Related Chords" (also in the April '78 issue of *GP).*

For those who don't have the April issue, I'll say that for most purposes in actual playing situations, a mode is formed simply by taking a scale, such as the *G* scale, and instead of starting on the note *G,* you start from any other note in the scale and play up to the same note an octave higher. For example, you can start from *A* and play up the *G* scale to the *A* an octave higher (this results in an *A* dorian mode). Do the same for each of the remaining notes of the *G* scale, but remember that you are still playing in the key of *G* and must use the corresponding key signature of the original key (in the key of *G,* there is one sharp in the signature—*F*—so all *F*'s would be played as *F♯.* The following exercise shows the *G* scale in all of the modes that are based on it. All the fingerings are derived from the Form 1 scale fingerings. Each mode is named, and the chord symbols indicate the chord related to that particular mode:

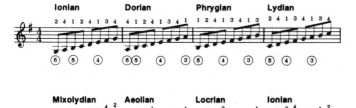

This next exercise is based on all of the chords that are derived from each mode. The chords are formed by taking the 1st, 3rd, 5th, and 7th notes from each mode. Incidentally, the mode is the improvising scale to be used for each chord. Notice once again that the fingerings come from the scale fingerings.

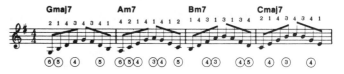

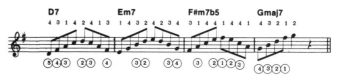

The following exercise combines the chords and the modes. You will play the ascending lines using the arpeggiated notes of the *chord,* and descend using the *mode* related to that chord.

All of the above exercises should be played up the fingerboard in all keys. That means if you start on the 2nd fret of the sixth string, you will be in the key of *G♭;* play all the exercises in *G♭.* If you start on the 3rd fret you will be in the key of *G*; starting from the 5th fret, you will be in the key of *A.* Continue through all the keys along the fingerboard.

I'd like to make a comment on the VII chord, derived from the locrian mode. I have at times called it a minor 7♭5, and at other times a half-diminished chord. Both ways are correct, and many times this chord form will be represented by the symbol ø. You may choose to call it either one.

Arnie Berle's
FRETBOARD BASICS

December 1978

Improvisation, Scales, And Modes, Part III

BEFORE GOING INTO THE SUBJECT MATTER FOR THIS MONTH I want to review just a bit of what was discussed in the past two columns, so that you can see the whole picture of where we're going. In the Oct. '78 issue of *GP*, I gave you a fingering for the major scale that, just as a means of identification, I called Form 1 fingering. Along with the scale itself, I included several exercises for developing a facility with it. These exercises were to be played up the entire fingerboard beginning with the $G\flat$ scale, played from the 2nd fret on the sixth string.

A jazz performer must have complete control and must be at ease playing in any key. A good exercise would be to take a scale and just "noodle" around on it so that you develop a good sense of its fingering. In the Nov. '78 column we showed how the modes are derived from scales and how the chords for each particular key are formed by using the various modes within the scale. Incidentally, for those of you who are thinking that these mode studies were very confining, I want to tell you that we will be learning two-octave modes all along the fingerboard later on. The reason why I'm restricting myself to playing all the modes in one position is to show you in a smaller scope what the jazz guitarist is doing when playing all over the board; the principles are exactly the same. Have patience, and we'll cover the whole thing.

Now that you've familiarized yourself with all the chords that can be played in one scale, let's concentrate on those very important chords that you've heard so much about, namely the II-V-I chords. In previous columns you played these chords in progressions all over the board in every key. Now let's look at these chords from the improviser's viewpoint. Once again we will use the *G* scale, Form 1 fingering as a source from which to draw all our examples. Below are the fingerings for the *Gmaj7* chord (in this case, the I chord); the *G6* chord fingerings are also given:

Here are the fingerings for the *Am7* chord, the II chord in the key of *G*:

Here are the fingerings for the *D7* chord, the V chord in the key of *G*:

All of the above chords may be extended to the 9th; below are the same chords with the added 9th.

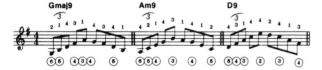

Since the II-V-I progression is used so frequently in so many tunes, it is very important for the jazz player to be thoroughly familiar with it in every key. Below are several patterns based on this sequence of chords. Again, you must play each pattern in every key up the fingerboard. The examples given are all in the key of *G*, using the Form 1 fingering. By moving your hand one fret higher on the fingerboard and using the same fingering as given below, you will be playing the II-V-I patterns in the key

of $A\flat$. Moving up another fret will put you into the key of *A*. Play right up the board. Later you will be given other fingerings:

This next pattern makes use of the modes indicated along with the chord symbols:

Each of the next few patterns covers two measures (at this point the string designations are omitted):

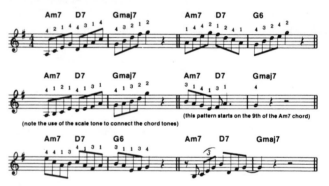

In many tunes there are long series of II-V chord progressions that don't resolve to the I chord until several measures have gone by. "Satin Doll" is an example of a tune that moves in series of II-V chords. Below are some II-V patterns:

Obviously the patterns shown above are very basic and are by no means examples of great jazz. The purpose of them is to get you acquainted with where they (or at least the notes which are used) are located on the fingerboard. You will be getting more progressions in future columns. Meantime, try to make up some on your own. It would be very helpful if you can get a friend to play the chords for you as you play through the patterns. You can also try recording the chords on a cassette recorder. When making up your own combinations, experiment with various rhythms, and also try placing scale tones in between the chord tones so that the patterns don't sound like chord exercises. Again, this will all be elaborated upon in future columns. The importance of acquiring many patterns based on the more common chord progressions cannot be stressed too emphatically. Every great jazz artist has any number of them that can be instantly drawn upon when the well of inspiration runs dry. In an interview I did with the great jazz guitarist Jimmy Raney [*GP* Mar. '77], he speaks about the need to build a collection of patterns which you can link together in various ways. He speaks at great length on the subject, and it would be well worth the time to dig up that interview. Till next time, keep practicing.

Arnie Berle's
FRETBOARD BASICS

Improvisation, Scales, And Modes, Part IV

IN THE NOVEMBER '78 COLUMN I SHOWED HOW THE MAJOR scale and all of its related modes may be played in one position. The example I used was the *G* major scale, played from the 3rd fret on the sixth string. I labeled the fingering Form 1. The purpose of this was to show how the improvising scales or the modes which are used to play on a II-V-I progression may be executed in one position. In the December '78 column I gave examples of II-V-I progressions in the key of *G*, and I used the notes of the *Am7* improvising scale (which is the *A* dorian mode) for the *Am7* chord. The *D* mixolydian mode was used as the improvising scale for the *D7* chord, and the *G* scale itself was used as the scale for the *Gmaj7* chord. All of these scales were played in the second position.

If you are wondering why I didn't use the *G* scale for the entire progression, rather than a different scale for each chord, the answer is that *I could have.* The *G* scale may be played throughout the entire *Am7-D7-Gmaj7* progression. However, by applying a different scale to the II chord and the V chord you are delaying the feeling of the tonic (I) so that when you finally get to the tonic chord, there is a feeling of arrival.

There is a natural tendency when playing on a scale to place more of an accent on certain notes. Usually these are the 1st, 3rd, 5th, and 7th scale tones, which are the notes of the tonic (I) chord. So when playing in the *A* dorian mode, for example, you will be stressing more notes compatible with the *Am7* chord than if you were utilizing the *G* scale (where you might stress more *G*'s, *B*'s, and *D*'s). However, let me emphasize right now that for anyone just getting into improvisation it is perfectly all right to play in the major scale of the I chord against the II-V-I progression. No one will say that you are playing "wrong" notes. The *G* scale will fit fine with the *Am7-D7-Gmaj7* progression. Playing in the key area or key center of a given progression is a perfectly acceptable way of improvising; you will never be considered wrong in doing so. But by using different scales for each chord you are giving your music more color, creating more interest to your solos. It is similar to using altered, extended, or substitute chords when playing a chord background.

Now let's see how to play the modes in different positions so that you can have a scale for each chord all the way up the fingerboard. Once again, we will use the key of *G* for our example. The following diagrams show all of the chords of the *G* scale with the mode or improvising scale for each chord. Each scale is shown in standard music notation and in a fingerboard diagram. I have also included the chord arpeggio for each mode. Notice that the fingering for the arpeggio comes directly from the scale fingering; if you wish to make adjustments in the finger placement, feel free to do so.

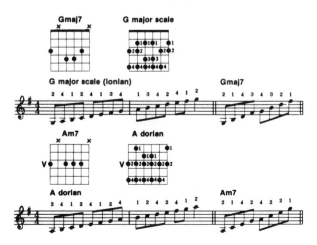

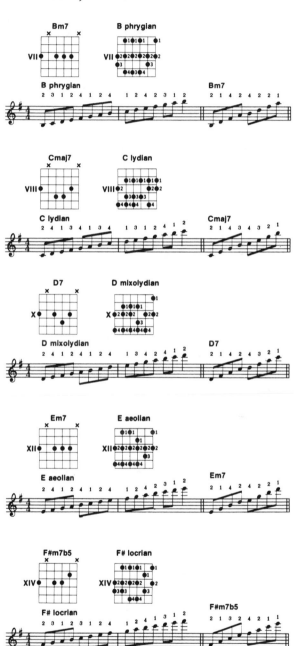

There you have it—all the improvising scales, or what we call modes, to match all the chords of the *G* scale. These fingerings will take some time to learn. Be patient; don't rush through them. I must say that in my private teaching I usually don't give these scales until much later than I have provided them in these columns. However since I have gotten so much mail on them, I decided to discuss them now. If you can't get them all by next month, don't worry; go on with the rest of the material and eventually it will all catch up. Next month I will show how to apply all the fingerings to other keys without having to run all over the fingerboard.

Arnie Berle's
FRETBOARD BASICS

February 1979

Playing Modes From The 3rd Fret

IN MY JANUARY '79 COLUMN I SHOWED HOW TO PLAY all of the modes, or improvising scales, for each chord of the *G* harmonized scale. We began with the obvious *G* scale for the *Gmaj7* chord, and then we went up to the 5th fret and played the *A* dorian mode to fit the *Am7* chord. Next we went to the 7th fret and played the *B* phrygian mode to fit the *Bm7 chord*. Finally, we went all the way up the fingerboard, playing the correct mode for each of the remaining chords of the key of *G*. Now I want to put all of these modes into a clearer perspective by playing them all from the *same* fret, which might help you to see them a bit better.

We will play all of the modes from the same tonic note—the *G* dorian mode, the *G* phrygian, *G* lydian, etc. This should aid in your understanding of the fingerings and the relationships between one mode and the next. As you learn each new mode, be sure to play it up the fingerboard. It is important that the fingering differences are felt, as well as understood. Once again, as a starting point we will begin with the *G* major scale, or the ionian mode. The chord form for each mode will also be given:

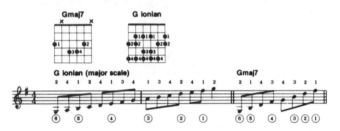

Next is the *G* dorian mode, which is a scale starting from the second note of the *F* major scale. The key signature contains one flat *(B♭)*. Another way of thinking of the dorian is to take the pure (natural) minor scale and raise the 6th step; this raised 6th gives the mode its distinctive sound. We will explore this further in a future column on modal harmony. For now, just think of the dorian mode as the scale starting from the second note of any major scale. It is the one used to improvise off of the II chord in a major key.

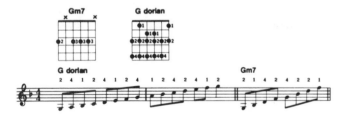

The *G* phrygian mode is the scale starting from the third note of the *E♭* scale; its key signature contains three flats *(B♭, E♭, A♭)*. Another way of thinking of the phrygian mode is to take the natural minor scale and lower the 2nd step. This scale is used to improvise off of a III chord in a major key.

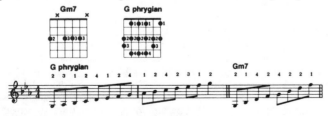

The *G* lydian mode is formed by playing a scale that starts on the 4th note of the *D* scale; it has two sharps *(F♯ and C♯)* in the key signature. Another way of visualizing it is to take the major scale and raise the 4th step.

Although it starts on the 4th note of the major scale, it is used by many jazz players to play off of the I chord in a major key.

The *G* mixolydian mode starts on the 5th note of the *C* scale. You can also think of the mixolydian mode as a major scale with a lowered 7th step. This scale can be used against a V7 chord in a major key.

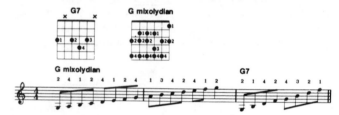

The *G* aeolian mode starts on the 6th step of the *B♭* scale, and has two flats *(B♭ and E♭)* in the key signature. It can be thought of as a pure, or natural, minor scale, and it is often used to improvise off of a VI chord in a major key.

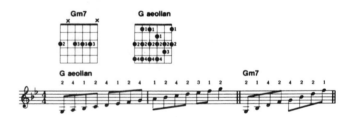

The *G* locrian mode starts on the 7th note of the *A♭* major scale. It may also be thought of as a pure minor scale with lowered 2nd and 5th steps. It's often used to improvise off of a minor 7th chord with a lowered 5th (m7♭5, or a half-diminished chord). The locrian is also called a half-diminished scale:

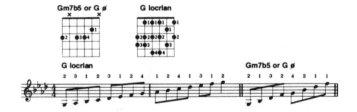

Now you have all of the modes played at the 3rd fret. Notice the differences in fingerings and listen carefully to the differences in sound quality. In past columns I have given patterns to play based on the major scales. They should now be played through all of the above modes so that you become familiar with the feel and sound of each mode. It is important that you understand that there are many other ways of playing each of the modes; there is no "one and only" way of fingering them. I simply used these fingerings for a comparison, and to show how it is possible to change from one mode to another within the same position by a slight alteration of the fingering. Next month we will cover modal harmony.

Arnie Berle's
FRETBOARD BASICS

March 1979

Modal Harmony

IN THE LAST SEVERAL COLUMNS I HAVE BEEN discussing the modes derived from the major scale and providing some fingerings for these different modes. The purpose was to show you what scale you might use when improvising to accompany a particular chord. For example, by now you should understand that you can play a *D* dorian mode for a *Dm7* chord, you can use the *G* mixolydian mode for a *G7* chord, and you can use the *C* ionian mode (the *C* major scale) for the *Cmaj7* chord. The three chords just mentioned represent the II-V-I progression in the key of *C* major.

Now I want to expand a bit on the modes, since they're sometimes used as the sole basis for entire musical compositions. In 1958 the great trumpet player Miles Davis recorded *Kind Of Blue* [Columbia, PC-8163]. That album was to change the course of jazz. On it were several compositions that were *not* based harmonically upon II-V-I progressions moving through several key centers (as had been the usual case up to that point). Instead, each structure rested on themes built upon specific modes.

One tune in particular, "So What," used a single modal scale for each eight-measure phrase; in other words, saxophonist John Coltrane had to improvise on a single mode for each set of eight measures. No longer was he required to play his way through a series of chords, but rather he could play on the one mode for eight measures. This was the first new concept in jazz improvisation since the advent of the bebop era, which went to the other extreme. In the bop era more chords were being used; chords were being extended and altered all over the place. Jazz players had all they could do to keep up with the harmonies, and the strain on their abilities really put them to the wall.

Of course, some of the older players couldn't cope with all the demands of bebop music, though many others accepted the challenge and went back to the woodshed to practice. Where they once had to just play through 7th chords and hope to come up with something interesting, the beboppers had to worry about playing through 9th chords, raised 11th chords, and 13th chords. Plus they sometimes had to worry about making sure they lowered and raised their 5ths and 9ths. Then, with just this one Miles Davis record, the demands on jazz players had changed again. Now musicians had the complete freedom to play all around in one mode or scale —not just for two or four counts, but for a full eight measures, or in some cases a whole tune of 32 measures. The Miles Davis album blew everyone's mind. Coltrane and many others such as Chick Corea, Herbie Hancock, McCoy Tyner, Joe Farrell, and Freddie Hubbard began writing compositions using modes as the basis for their music.

Along with the "freeing-up" of the soloist came new responsibilities for chord players such as keyboardists and guitarists. A chord player couldn't just sit there any play, say, a *Cm7* chord for all those long periods of time that someone was soloing in *C* dorian. Instead he had to go back and study the modes and see what harmonies he could play that would *enhance* the solo while also reinforcing the sound of the mode. (This was somewhat similar to playing II-V-I changes when working in major and minor keys.)

Bear in mind that while all this was very new for the jazz players, it wasn't new for the people involved with classical music. The modes have been around since before 1600— almost all "serious" music was once associated with religion, and the modes were sometimes referred to as the church or ecclesiastical modes. It was a gradual process that led to the emergence of the ionian (major) and aeolian (with harmonic and melodic forms) modes as the two principal tonal systems used in composition. However, since the late '50s, with the release of *Kind Of Blue* paving the way, many contemporary compositions are now being written utilizing the various other modes such as dorian, phrygian, lydian, and mixolydian. The locrian mode is generally not used because it lacks a strong, stable quality due to the tritone relationship between the 1st and 5th scale steps:

Some of the popular tunes that utilize modal qualities are "My Favorite Things" (of which Coltrane has an excellent recording on *Mastery Of John Coltrane,* Impulse, 9345), "Taste Of Honey," "Love For Sale," "It Ain't Necessarily So," "Norwegian Wood," "Misirlou," and "Greensleeves." Modal compositions by jazz artists include "Moon Germs," "Times Lie," and "Great Gorge" from the Joe Farrell album *Moon Germs* [CTI, 6023]. An LP by Gil Evans called *Out Of The Blue* [Impulse, S-4] contains "La Nevada" and "Sunken Treasure." Freddie Hubbard's album *The Artistry Of Freddie Hubbard* on Impulse [S-27] includes "Caravan," "Summertime," and "The Seventh Hour"—all modal pieces.

The works cited above should serve as a good introduction to modal compositions. In my next column I will acquaint you with other tunes, and we'll explore modal harmonies and various chords that may be used to comp behind someone who is playing a solo based on a particular mode.

Arnie Berle's
FRETBOARD BASICS

Primary Chords Of Modes, Part I

IN LAST MONTH'S COLUMN I SPOKE ABOUT A TURNING POINT IN THE history of jazz—an album by trumpeter Miles Davis released in 1958 called *Kind Of Blue* [Columbia, PC-8163]. On it was a song called "So What," which was to change the direction of jazz. For the first time, a tune was recorded that was built on a particular scale known as the dorian mode, or dorian scale.

This wasn't the usual II-V chord progression moving through several keys so popular at the time (a result of all the work of the beboppers during the 1940s). Rather, here was a tune constructed on one chord, *Dm7*, and John Coltrane (who played sax on the album) was able to improvise over the dorian scale for the entire solo.

It wasn't long before this concept of modal playing became the model for a number of jazz stars such as keyboardists Herbie Hancock, Chick Corea, and Keith Jarrett (among others). Coltrane himself became very involved in modal playing with his own groups, and he released an album called "Love Supreme" (Impulse (dist. by ABC), 77]. It included the composition "Persuance." Another modal piece that Coltrane did was his very successful "My Favorite Things" [from *The Mastery Of John Coltrane*, Impulse, 9345].

Now, the question is: What chords are being used while the soloist is playing his lines? We know that in standard arrangements, supporting musicians are feeding chords characteristic of the particular key or keys that the tune is going through; In other words, they might play the II and V chords of each new key. A good example is Duke Ellington's "Satin Doll' [see my May '78 *GP* column for the chord progressions]. The tune goes through the keys of *C, D, G,* and *G♭*; in the bridge it goes into the key of F. The chord player is using the II and V chords in each of these keys. This approach is fine for major and minor songs, but what does the chord player do when the tune is constructed on one modal scale?

Since there are six different modes (excluding the ionian mode, which is the major scale), there are six different sets of chords which must be learned. Each mode has its own characteristic, or primary, chords.

The dorian mode. The dorian mode up to this point has been presented in this column as the one beginning on the second note of the major scale. You can improvise in the dorian when playing the II chord of the II-V progression, but in terms of modal harmony and extended compositions based on the mode, we have to adjust our thinking a bit. Think now of the dorian mode as the scale created by *raising the 6th note* of the natural minor scale by one half-step:

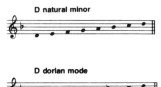

The key signature of the dorian is the same as the major scale built one whole-step below the tonic of the dorian. In other words, the key signature of the *D* dorian mode would be the same as the *C* major scale. However, in most compositions written in the dorian mode, the signature given is usually that of the parallel minor key. Therefore, the *D* dorian mode would have the same key signature as *D* minor (the raised 6th, *B*-natural, is shown as an accidental).

It is this raised 6th step of the scale that gives the dorian mode its distinctive quality. A melody based on the dorian should contain the raised 6th in order to maintain the flavor of the mode:

Chords are formed from the mode in the same way that they are derived from the major key—by building intervals of thirds over each note of the mode:

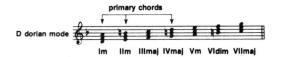

The primary chords of the dorian mode are the I (tonic), the II, and the IV: The II and IV contain the raised 6th note. Although the VI chord also contains the raised 6th, it is a diminished chord, and its use would tend to take a composition out of its key. Therefore, it is generally excluded from consideration as a primary chord.

Any combination of the I, II, and IV chords may be used to harmonize a dorian-based improvised melody; these are used to comp behind the soloist. You can use combinations of the I-II or I-IV, but it's always a good idea to end on the I.

The phrygian mode. The phrygian mode is formed by lowering the 2nd step of the natural minor scale. This lowered 2nd note gives the mode its characteristic flavor.

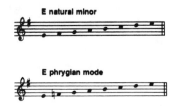

The phrygian mode is built on the 3rd note of a major scale and takes its key signature from the 1st note in that same scale. For example, the *E* phrygian mode would have the same key signature as the *C* major scale. But again, in most phrygian-based compositions written today, the key signature would be the same as that of the parallel minor key. So, *E* phrygian would have the same key signature as *E* minor (there is one sharp—*F♯*—in the signature). The lowered 2nd step, *F*-natural, would be indicated as an accidental. It is the lowered 2nd step that should be used in any melody based on the phrygian mode:

Below are the chords formed from the phrygian mode. The primary chords are I (tonic), II, and VII. The II and the VII contain the lowered 2nd step. Any combination of these chords may be used to comp behind a soloist improvising in this mode:

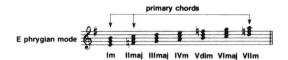

Next month we'll continue with the rest of the modes, and I'll also give an example of a modal composition. This piece will be from the album *White Trees* [Chiaroscuro (221 W. 57th St., New York, NY 10019), CR-193], by Mike Santiago and Entity. I'll also show the chord forms that Mike used on it. In the meantime, try to digest what I've just given you. If you have any questions, feel free to write me c/o *GP*, and I'll try to answer them in a future column.

Primary Chords Of Modes, Part II

LAST MONTH WE DISCUSSED THE PRIMARY CHORDS OF THE DORIAN and phrygian modes. These chords would be similar to the I, II, and V chords of the major scale. (Incidentally, the major scale is also called the ionian mode.) Now I want to continue with the primary chords for the rest of the modes.

The lydian mode. The lydian mode is formed by raising the 4th step of the major scale. This raised 4th step is the note that gives the mode its characteristic flavor:

The key signature of the lydian mode is the same as that of the major scale that begins on the note a perfect fifth above the lydian's tonic (l). In other words, the key signature of the C lydian mode would be the same as that of the G major scale (one sharp—F♯), since G is a fifth above C. However, in popular usage most compositions written in the lydian mode employ the same key signature as that of the parallel major scale. In this case, the C lydian mode would use the same key signature as the C major scale, and the raised 4th would be indicated as an accidental.

Any melody based on the lydian mode should contain the raised 4th, in order to maintain the flavor of the mode:

Below are the chords formed from the lydian mode. The chords which contain the raised 4th become the primary chords for the mode. It should be noted that the I chord, which doesn't contain the raised 4th, is considered a primary chord, as it establishes the key: the II and the VII chords are the other two primary chords of the lydian mode. Notice that although the IV chord also contains the raised 4th step, it is a *diminished* chord and contains the *tritone*. The use of that chord would tend to weaken the mode and demand resolution to a chord built on the fifth note of the mode, rather than the tonic of the mode. Therefore it isn't considered as a primary chord (see the example below):

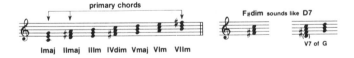

The mixolydian mode. The mixolydian mode is formed by lowering the 7th step of the major scale. This lowered 7th step is the note that gives the mode its characteristic flavor:

The key signature of the mixolydian mode is the same as the major scale built a perfect 4th above the mixolydian mode's tonic. In other words, the key signature of the C mixolydian mode would be the same as the F major scale (one flat—B♭. However, in popular usage music written in the mixolydian mode uses the key signature of the parallel major scale, and the lowered 7th is shown as an accidental. So the C mixolydian mode uses the key signature of the C major scale, but the lowered 7th note is indicated as an accidental. The following melody contains the lowered 7th step, which is necessary in order to maintain the flavor of the mode:

Below are the chords formed from the mixolydian mode. The primary chords for this mode are the chords which contain the lowered 7th note: the V and VII chords. The tonic chord is also included as a primary chord, even though it does not have a lowered 7th. Although the III chord contains the lowered 7th. It is a diminished chord, and contains the tritone. Its use as a primary chord would weaken the mode: therefore, it's excluded.

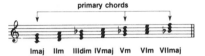

The aeolian mode. The aeolian mode is another name for the natural minor scale, and it has the same key signature as its relative major scale. The differences between the aeolian mode and the more commonly used minor scales (harmonic and melodic) are the natural 6th and 7th steps:

Any melody written in the aeolian mode should contain the natural 6th and 7th steps in order to differentiate the mode from the traditional minor scales:

Below are the chords formed from the aeolian mode. Those which contain the natural 6th and 7th steps tend to reinforce the aeolian mode. Those chords which are most used are the I (to establish the key), V, VI, and VII.

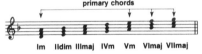

The locrian mode. The locrian mode is the least used of all the modes because of the diminished quality of its I (tonic) chord. This diminished quality, as I said earlier, tends to weaken the feeling of the tonic chord. The mode is used as an improvising scale for the *m7♭5* chord.

*   *   *   *

We have now completed outlining the primary chords of the modes, with the exception of the locrian mode, which we will cover in a future column. I want to make several things clear: First, just as in the major scale, you are also allowed to make use of chromatic tone when using any of the modes. Second, it is not always necessary to play the characteristic notes of the mode in the melody, as long as they are included in the chordal harmony. Third, chords other than triads may be used (and often are used), but again, care must be taken not to weaken the modal feeling. Fourth, just as in compositions written in the major key, you can use chromatic chords in modal playing.

In next month's column we will continue with the modes, and I'll show how triads may be placed over each other to form larger chords. I'll also demonstrate how to play these chords on the guitar.

Arnie Berle's
FRETBOARD BASICS

October 1979

More Readers' Questions

LAST MONTH I ANSWERED SOME COMMON QUESTIONS from readers. I would like to continue now with some more that we couldn't fit in last month's article. In case you're wondering how I choose the questions to be answered, I single out those that best typify what most of the guitarists ask. I usually devote an entire column or series of columns to those that require an answer that is long or detailed, as I did with the columns on the modes [Jan.-Aug. '79] (those came about because of great reader interest in that topic). Last month I listed some of the books I've published, in response to so many inquiries. Now let's shed some light on other topics.

There have been a number of letters from readers inquiring about the use of Roman numerals. Quite simply they are numbers assigned to each scale step (or each chord built on the members of a scale; see my May '78 *GP* column). The use of Roman numerals makes it easy for a musician to take a certain sequence of chords and conveniently transpose it from one key to another. For example, suppose you are in a band and the leader asks you to play a certain tune in a key other than the one you have been playing in. By knowing the numerical designation of each chord in the familiar key, it becomes a simple matter of transposing the *numerals* into the chords of the new key. Here is an example of how this is done: If the chords are *Cmaj7, Am7, Dm7,* and *G7* in the key of *C*, then their corresponding Roman numerals would be I, VI, II, and V. By transposing the Roman numerals to the key of *G*, and playing the same sequence, the chords would be *Gmaj7, Em7, Am7* and *D7* (again, I, VI, II, and V, but in the new key).

Transposition from one major key to another is easier if you know that in traditional jazz the I chord is virtually always a major 7th chord; the VI and II chords are minor 7th chords; and the V chord is a dominant 7th chord (the word "dominant" is omitted in the chord symbol).

From John Gibson of Brandon, Manitoba, came a question about the use of Roman numerals in representing chords in the harmonized scale. John suggests that the minor chords are better represented as lower case. For example, in the key of *C*, the Roman numeral representation of *Dm7* would be ii rather than II, or the *Am7* would be vi rather than VI, etc. Well, some writers do use lower case numerals, so you should know about it. I have nothing against their use; however, when referring to chords in the harmonized major scale, the II, III, and the VI chord are minor. Therefore, it shouldn't be necessary to use a special designation for those chords.

Vincent Coady of Victoria, British Columbia, wanted to know of some beginning improvisational approaches. This is another common question, and I will address the subject in later columns; for now I'll try to make my reply very short. First of all, you should be able to play the basic major scales. (It is not necessary to know all the various minor scales and all the modes at the very beginning stages, in spite of all you have been reading about them.) You should

also be able to play through the major and minor chords. Of course, learning the other chords, such as diminished, augmented, and the various altered chords is important too, but remember, you don't have to know them before you start to improvise. Nonetheless, as you progress, you will want to know these other chords so that you can improvise better.

One way to get started is to take a slow, standard type of tune such as "I'm In The Mood For Love." Any slow-moving tune will do, as long as there are notes in the melody that last for two or more beats. Play the melody, and at those points where the melody note is being held for more than one count, begin to play little melodic fill-ins. You can use notes from the chords and play up or down on those tones. Gradually you can add notes between the chord tones, but keep your fills simple and easy; don't try to throw in everything you know. Make sure your fill-ins occupy the correct number of beats. At the same time you can change the values of the original melody notes; that is, wherever you have two quarter notes, you can make the first one a dotted quarter note and the second note an eighth-note. Try to make the rhythm of the original melody more interesting. Start to play *around* the melody, but don't stray too far from it. And always know where you are in the tune.

As you do this with more songs you can take more liberties, and as you begin to improvise better you can try to use other chords in place of the original ones. Then learn the more colorful scales to use against the given chords. These newer scales will add more tensions or more interest to your improvisation. I have included many improvisational techniques in my book, *The Complete Handbook For Jazz Improvisation* [Music Sales Corp. (33 W. 60th St., New York, NY 10023)]. It may help to guide you through some of the various approaches to improvising. In my private teaching I use several different approaches, depending on the student, his background, how much he knows, and his ability. But the method I have outlined in this column is as good a beginning as any.

Here is a question from Gary Tunheim, of Thief River Falls, Minnesota. He asks about the fingering for the melodic minor scale. The best thing I can say about that for now is to simply play any major scale you know and lower the third note. For example, in *C* melodic minor, play *C, D, E♭, F, G, A, B,* and *C.* Lowering that third note will automatically produce the melodic minor scale. Jazz players generally only use the ascending form of the melodic minor scale, so that little rule I just gave you should do the job. I'll get further into the mechanics of the melodic minor scale in a future column.

Well, once again it's time to wrap my column up for the month. I want to thank you all for the many letters you've sent and for all the nice words. I hope you will keep writing and asking questions. Till next month, "straight ahead."

Arnie Berle's
FRETBOARD BASICS

November 1979

Playing Scales In One Position

IN MY LAST TWO COLUMNS I TRIED TO ANSWER SOME of the questions asked by many readers. I chose questions that required only brief answers, but for the next several columns I will try to cover a much-requested topic that necessitates a greater amount of elaboration: scales and their fingerings.

It seems that the most confusion arises in how to finger the scales. On no other instrument is the question of scale fingering as confusing as on the guitar. On the flute, saxophone, clarinet, and piano (just to name a few), there is only one way to finger any given scale. But on the guitar there are several ways to play every scale. Each can be played at a number of different locations on the fingerboard, so I'll try to cover these in the next several months.

My October '78 column was based on one way to finger scales in which the keynote, or tonic, began on the sixth string. I'd like to review part of that for you, and then demonstrate how to finger the same scales—this time starting from the fifth string. At the time I called this fingering Form 1—simply an arbitrary way of identifying it. Here it is again:

Notice that the notes within the brackets indicate those that are still in the same key, but are either below or above the tonic note. Here is a diagram showing the fingering for those who do not read standard music notation:

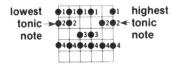

The following table shows the names of the scales that begin at each fret on the sixth string (starting with the 2nd fret):

Fret	2	3	4	5	6	7	8	9	10	11	12	13
Scale	Gb F#	G	Ab	A	Bb	B	C	Db C#	D	Eb	E	F

Now I would like to show you how to finger the major scales with their tonics on the *fifth* string. I will start with the *C* major scale, starting from the 3rd fret. For purposes of identification, we will call this the Form 2 fingering. Notice also the bracketed notes indicating that the scale can be extended below the tonic, down onto the sixth string.

This next diagram represents the fingering for the scale I just showed. Notice that it is necessary to go out of the original hand position in order to play a full two-octave scale.

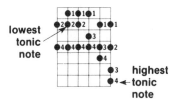

Here is a table showing the starting note (tonic) of each scale that begins on the fifth string:

Fret	2	3	4	5	6	7	8	9	10	11	12	13
Scale	B	C	Db C#	D	Eb	E	F	Gb F#	G	Ab	A	Bb

With the two fingerings I have shown (Form 1 and Form 2), you can play each major scale at two locations on the fingerboard. Below is an exercise based on all of the major scales. The number in the circle above each scale name indicates which fingering you might use. For example, play the C major scale starting at the 8th fret on the sixth string; then play the F major scale starting at the 8th fret on the fifth string. Continue in the same way through the entire exercise. Play each scale only from the lowest tonic note to the highest tonic note; in other words, do not play the bracketed notes. In this way you will hear the true sound of the scale. Later, when you gain more proficiency, you may want to go beyond the two-octave boundaries.

In case you are wondering why the Form 2 fingering requires you to move out of position, it is only necessary to do so if you want to play the full two octaves. Otherwise, you can keep your hand in one place and still have enough notes to improvise with.

Having just completed the exercise above, you should begin to realize that it's possible to play in two keys while keeping your hand in the same position. For example, while in the second position, you can play in the keys of C and G; in the third you can play in the keys of Ab and Db etc. In future columns you will learn how to play in six different keys while keeping your hand in the same position.

19

Arnie Berle's
FRETBOARD BASICS

December 1979

More Scale Fingerings

LAST MONTH I GAVE YOU TWO MAJOR-SCALE FINGER-ings, which we called Form 1 and Form 2. Before I mention any more scale fingerings, I want to present a series of exercises that will help you to develop fluency with the fingerings you already know. Below are several exercises, all written in the key of C; each has two sets of fingerings, Form 1 and Form 2. If you play all exercises with the lowest tonic note (*C*) on the sixth string, you will use the Form 1 fingering. If you play an exercise with the tonic note on the fifth string, you will use the Form 2 fingering. For greatest benefit, each exercise should be played in every key up the fingerboard.

Even though the fingerings remain the same from key to key, the feel of the fingerboard changes as the frets get closer together (toward the bridge) and farther apart (toward the nut). Follow the order of scales that I gave you last month: that is, *C, F, B♭, E♭, A♭*, etc. This will help you to know the fingerboard better—the ultimate goal—so that you can play patterns all over the fingerboard in any key. The fingerings are given in the first three examples. By the time you get to Ex. 4, you should be able to work out your own. Be sure to make allowances for the higher notes of the Form 2 fingering.

This is important: Fingerings may vary from player to player because of the difference in the size of each person's hand. So don't be afraid to use a fingering that may vary from what I've given if what you use is more comfortable. As you learn more scale finger-ings in the next few columns, you may discover a better way to finger some of the patterns that now seem awkward—particularly those played on the first two strings using the Form 2 fingerings. Above all, don't become your own worst enemy: Practice slowly, and even the most awkward fingerings can be overcome. Till next month, "straight ahead."

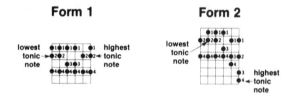

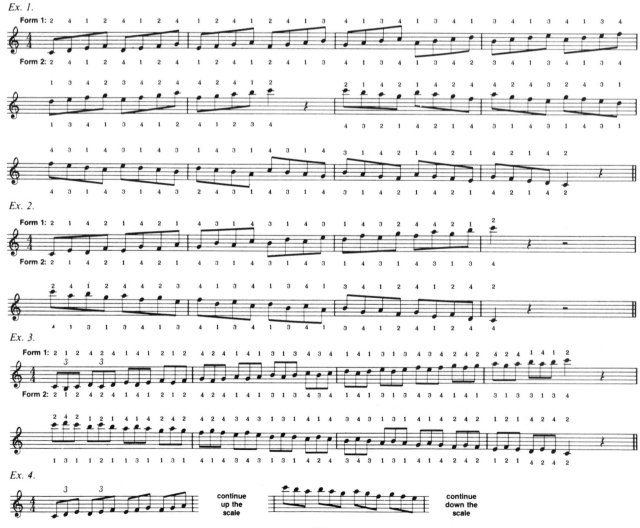

Arnie Berle's
FRETBOARD BASICS

Two More Major Scale Approaches

IN MY NOVEMBER '79 COLUMN I GAVE YOU THE fingerings for major scales whose tonic notes were located on the sixth string. I arbitrarily called the necessary fingering Form 1, simply as a means of identification. I also provided a fingering for the major scales whose tonics are on the fifth string and called that fingering pattern Form 2. Now I want to list two more fingerings for the major scale.

This first fingering, which we will call Form 3, has its tonic note on the sixth string. The example shows the *A* major scale starting at the 5th fret on the sixth string. The notes in brackets are also contained in the key, but there are not enough notes to make up another complete scale.

Here is a diagram of the Form 3 scale fingering:

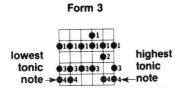

The following is a table showing each scale (beginning from the 5th fret) that results as you play up the fingerboard:

Fret	5	6	7	8	9	10	11	12	13	14	15	16
Scale	A	Bb	B	C	Db C#	D	Eb	E	F	Gb F#	G	Ab

Another fingering for the major scale whose tonic note begins on the fifth string we will call Form 4; the example shown here is the *D* major scale. Notice that it does not allow a full two-octave scale to be played. (Remember that the notes contained within the brackets are in the key, but are not of sufficient number to complete another scale.)

The fingering for the Form 4 scale is shown in this diagram:

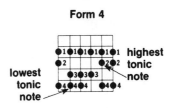

The table shows each scale (beginning from the 5th fret) played at each fret along the fingerboard.

Fret	5	6	7	8	9	10	11	12	13	14	15	16
Scale	D	Eb	E	F	Gb F#	G	Ab	A	Bb	B	C	Db C#

The following exercise is based on only the Form 3 and Form 4 scale fingerings. Do not use the Form 1 and Form 2 fingerings that you learned in the November '79 column. We will use all the forms together later on. The letter over each measure tells which scale is to be played; the number in the circle tells which scale fingering to use. For example, in measure 1, play the *C* scale using the Form 3 fingering starting at the 8th fret. Then play the *F* scale starting from the 8th fret using the Form 4 fingering. For the purpose of this exercise play each scale only from the lowest tonic note. Do not play the notes in the brackets; you will hear the true scale sound if they are excluded. For the Form 4 scale you *can* play the higher bracketed notes, since they shouldn't obscure the sound of the scale.

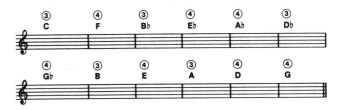

Remember that the above exercises are only to illustrate where these scales may be played on the fingerboard. Later on, you will see by combining all the forms that it is possible to stay in one position and play many of these scales that presently seem so far out of the way. Till next month, "straight ahead."

Arnie Berle's
FRETBOARD BASICS

Scale Fingering Options

IN THE JANUARY '80 COLUMN I GAVE YOU TWO FINGER-ings for major scales which began on the fifth and sixth strings with the 4th finger. I called the scale fingerings Form 3 (it starts on the sixth string) and Form 4 (which begins on the fifth). The form numbers are arbitrary—they just distinguish one from another. In the November '79 column I illustrated Forms 1 and 2; be sure to keep reviewing these forms all over the fingerboard.

Now I want to show you a series of exercises based on Forms 3 and 4. For the first one (Form 3 fingering) I chose to put the exercise in the key of A, which starts with the 4th finger on the 5th fret of the sixth string. The reason for using the key of A is simply that many guitar students may find it easier to read at the lower part of the neck. After you learn the pattern, it's just a matter of placing your 4th finger anywhere on the sixth string and repeating the pattern from that point. Here is the exercise:

Notice the alternate fingering (shown in parentheses); the use of the 4th finger on the fourth string eliminates some of the awkwardness of having to use the 1st finger while crossing strings and moving one fret over. However, the alternate fingering is optional, and its use depends on the sequence of notes being played. The first exercise should be played in every key whose tonic note lies on the sixth string. If you have a long enough fingerboard, play through the entire cycle.

Here is another exercise that should be played using the Form 3 fingering. Again, the exercise is shown in the key of A so that it is easier to read. This time the fingering notations are eliminated. It should also be played at all positions along the fingerboard.

This next exercise is based on the scale fingering called Form 4, and it is in the key of D, starting with the 4th finger at the 5th fret on the fifth string. Again, this is shown at the lower part of the fingerboard in order to make it easier to read. When you can play the exercise well and have memorized the pattern, play it in all keys whose tonic notes fall on the fifth string.

For additional exercises, refer back to my column in the December '79 issue of GP. Those patterns should also be played using the new Form 3 and Form 4 fingerings. It's important to play as many exercises as you can using all of the various scale fingerings. I would like to thank my publisher, Music Sales [33 West 60th St., New York, NY 10023], for allowing me to use some of this material from my book *Fretboard Fundamentals*.

Next month I'll give you two more scale fingerings, and then we'll learn how to connect them all so that you can play everywhere on the fingerboard. Till then, "straight ahead."

Arnie Berle's
FRETBOARD BASICS

Two More Scale Fingerings

IN THE NOVEMBER '79 COLUMN I GAVE YOU TWO fingerings for the major scale. I called them Form 1 (which began with the 2nd finger on the sixth string) and Form 2 (which began with the 2nd finger on the fifth string). The January '80 column had two more scale fingerings; I called these Form 3 (which began with the 4th finger on the sixth string) and Form 4 (which began with the 4th finger on the fifth string).

Now I want to complete the series with two more fingering patterns, Form 5 and Form 6. You will then have six ways of fingering the major scale. One advantage is that in any one position you will be able to play in six different keys.

Here is the Form 5 scale fingering in two octaves. The notes within the brackets are contained in the key, but do not make up an additional octave. This example uses the F major scale:

The diagram below shows the fingering of Form 5 starting with the 1st finger on the sixth string:

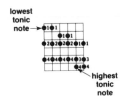

The table below shows the name of the scale starting at each fret along the sixth string.

1	2	3	4	5	6	7	8	9	10	11	12
F	F#/Gb	G	Ab	A	Bb	B	C	C#/Db	D	Eb	E

Below is a fingering for the major scale whose tonic note is found on the fifth string (it's played with the 1st finger). We will call this pattern Form 6 (compare it to Form 2, which begins on the same string with the 2nd finger). Remember that the notes in the brackets are contained in the key, but there aren't enough of them to make up another complete octave. The scale in this example is Bb major.

Here's a diagram of the Form 6 fingering:

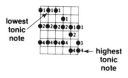

This next table shows which key begins at each of the frets along the sixth string.

1	2	3	4	5	6	7	8	9	10	11	12
Bb	B	C	C#/Db	D	Eb	E	F	F#/Gb	G	Ab	A

Now let's play the new scale fingerings through the cycle of fourths, beginning with the C scale played at the 8th fret on the sixth string. The numbers in the circles over each measure indicate which fingering to use. For the purposes of this study do *not* play the bracketed notes included with the Form 6 scale fingerings right away. It's always best to start a scale from its tonic note so that you get the sound of the scale in your ear. If you start with the bracketed notes, you can lose the feeling of the key. Once you're familiar with the sound of each scale, then add the bracketed notes.

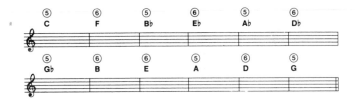

I hope you are still practicing the other scale forms that you learned in the past columns. If you are, the following study will be a good review for you. It shows the scales played through the cycle of fourths again, but it makes use of all six fingerings. The numbers in circles over each measure indicate which scale fingering to use.

Keep practicing, and until next month, "straight ahead."

23

Arnie Berle's
FRETBOARD BASICS

Connecting Scale Forms

IF YOU HAVE BEEN FOLLOWING MY COLUMNS SINCE November '79, you should now be well-acquainted with the six major scale fingerings (forms) and some of their alternates (see last month's column). At this point, I'd like to talk about how to connect these scale fingerings so that it's possible to play in one area, or position, of the fingerboard and then move smoothly to another area while remaining the same key. This could prove helpful in sight-reading, where you start out playing a line that contains primarily low notes, and then find it necessary to play a series of high notes.

Alternatively, you might find it more practical to shift to another position for the sake of easier fingering or a better sound. Let's just say that knowing how to connect one fingering to another while remaining in the same scale will improve your overall picture of the fingerboard.

The following examples show how the various scale forms may be connected. Let's begin with the Form 1 fingering (see my column for Nov. '79) in the key of G. Notice the half-step shift by the 1st finger; this puts you in position to play the key of G using the Form 5 fingering (see my March '80 column).

This next example shows the Form 5 fingering of the G scale connected to the Form 4 (Jan. '80) G scale. Notice the 1st-finger shift on the third string: it covers a whole-step. Make the transition as smooth as possible. In this example, I've included the string markings so that you can check yourself out as you play:

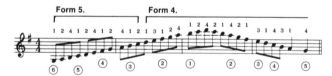

In this next example, the Form 4 G scale connects to the Form 2 (Nov. '79) G scale by using a stretch of the 4th finger on the third string.

To join the Form 2 fingering to Form 3 (Jan. '80), we'll use the key of D, since it is easy to visualize its notes which lie at the lower end of the fingerboard. Notice the shift of the 1st finger on the third string: it's a half-step, or one-fret, shift.

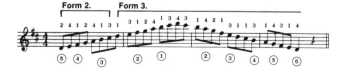

Here we will use the A scale, and see how the alternate Form 3a can be connected to Form 1. Notice the 4th-finger stretch on the fourth string.

Below we have the B♭ scale using Form 6 connected to a Form 1 B♭ scale. Notice the shift on the third string—a whole-step, or two-fret, shift. Play this as smoothly as possible.

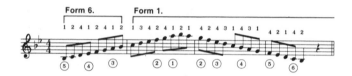

The following study is in the key of C: it moves through four different scale fingerings while remaining in the same key. Notice that the Form 3 fingering also makes use of the alternate fingering 3a in order to make the connection to Form 1.

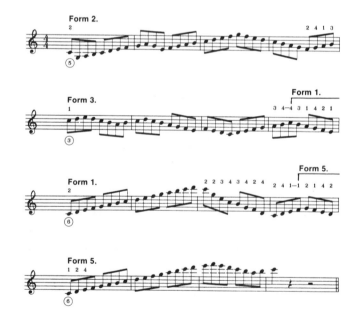

All of the above scale fingerings should be practiced in the combinations shown. For example, connect Form 1 to Form 5, Form 5 to Form 4, etc. Until next month, "straight ahead."

Arnie Berle's
FRETBOARD BASICS

Minor Scales, Part I

FOR THE PAST SEVERAL MONTHS WE'VE BEEN WORK-ing with major scales and six different fingerings that could be used for each of them. I must say that it's been most gratifying to see the response from readers who have written to me, met me in music stores, or called me on the phone. The interest in scales appears to be greater than ever, and I suppose it's because of the increasing desire to improvise skillfully. Also, more and more guitarists realize the tremendous importance of scale knowledge in nearly every type of music.

Of course, the problem of playing scales on the guitar is greater than playing scales on just about any other instrument because of the duplication of notes on the fretboard. In other words, a single note can be played in several different locations.

Since November 1979 I have shown that any major scale can be played using six different fingerings. (I'm sure that many of you have even come up with other fingerings that I didn't cover.) So now that we have established a sense of direction with major scales, let's start working with the minor scales.

Every major scale has a relative minor scale, and the tonic (keynote, or starting note) of that minor scale is the sixth note of its relative major key. For example, the sixth note of the C major scale is A. Therefore, the relative minor scale for C major is A minor:

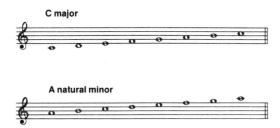

The minor scale is related to the major key because they share the same key signature. There are three forms to the minor scale: *natural* minor (shown above), *harmonic* minor, and *melodic* minor. Let's study their characteristics.

The natural minor scale, which is also called the *aeolian mode,* contains only the notes from the relative major scale; there are no alterations.

To form the harmonic minor scale, you must raise the seventh note of the natural minor scale. Note that this raised seventh is not indicated in the key signature, but instead as an accidental (sharp, flat, or natural sign) in the music itself:

A melodic minor scale is formed when you raise both the sixth and seventh notes of a natural minor scale as you ascend; these two notes are lowered to the same as those in natural minor when you descend:

The preceding form of the melodic minor scale is the classically accepted form. However, in recent years the melodic minor scale has been used extensively by jazz players, and a slight modification has been introduced. Called the *jazz minor* scale, it has raised sixth and seventh notes in both the ascending and descending forms.

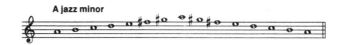

The reason that the melodic minor scale has gained such popularity among jazz players is that when it's played against a dominant 7th chord it provides altered notes such as the lowered 9th, raised 9th, lowered 5th, and raised 5th. These altered notes create the very modern sound that was one of the characteristics of bebop music. To find the correct *jazz* minor scale to play against any dominant 7th chord, just use the scale whose tonic note is a *half-step higher than* the root of the dominant 7th chord. For example, with an $E\flat 7$ chord, you would play an *E jazz* minor scale. This is shown below. The numbers under each note of the scale indicate its relationship to the $E\flat 7$ chord. For instance, the $\flat 9$ means that the note E is the lowered 9th of the $E\flat 7$, the $\sharp 9$ means that the $F\sharp$ is the raised 9th of the $E\flat 7$, etc.

Other chords which work well with the jazz minor scale as a basis for improvisation are the minor raised 7th ($m\sharp 7$) and the minor 6th (m6) chords. These use the jazz minor scale whose tonic note is the *same* as the root of the chord. For example, with a $Cm\sharp 7$ chord use the *C jazz* minor scale. For the *Cm6* chord also use the *C jazz* minor scale. The harmonic minor scale is used *only* with the minor raised 7th chord.

At this point, you should write out all the relative minor scales for each major scale. For those interested in further study (beyond this column) of minor scales, I discuss them in my book, *Fretboard Fundamentals* [Music Sales, 33 W. 60th St., New York, NY 10023]. Next month I will give you fingerings for the different minor scales. Until then, "straight ahead."

Arnie Berle's
FRETBOARD BASICS

Harmonic Minor Fingerings

IN LAST MONTH'S COLUMN, WE DISCUSSED THE THREE different forms of the minor scale: natural, harmonic, and melodic. We also saw how they are related to the major scale. Let's briefly review what we learned. Every major scale has a relative minor scale which starts from the 6th step of that major scale. For example, the relative minor scale for *C* major is *A* minor (the 6th note of the *C* scale is *A*).

Although all three forms of the minor scale observe the key signature of the relative major scale, let's see how the three forms differ. In the key of *A* minor, the *A* natural minor scale contains no alterations. The *A* harmonic minor scale has its 7th degree raised a half-step. The *A* melodic minor scale has its 6th and 7th degrees raised a half-step as the scale ascends. The *F* and *G* become *F♯* and *G♯*. But as the scale descends the 6th and 7th degrees return to their original form.

There is one further minor scale, called the jazz minor; it is simply the ascending version of the melodic minor scale, with the raised 6th and 7th degrees retained in both ascending and descending directions. (See my June 1980 column for further explanation of the jazz minor scale.)

This month we will focus on fingerings for the harmonic minor scale. The following ones start with the 2nd finger. We can label the fingerings as we did the major scales (see my Nov. '79, Dec.'79, and Jan. '80 columns). Thus, we will call the scale formation starting on the sixth string the Form 1 Minor, and the scale formation beginning on the fifth string Form 2 Minor. Remember that this is just an arbitrary way of identifying the scale fingerings for the purpose of learning them on the guitar. Here is the *A* harmonic minor scale using the Form 1 Minor fingering:

We'll use the *D* harmonic minor scale that starts on the fifth string to illustrate Form 2 Minor fingering:

The following fingerboard diagrams illustrate the fingerings for the Form 1 Minor and Form 2 Minor scales for those who don't read standard music notation:

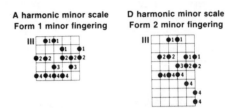

Both minor scale fingerings should be practiced in all the minor keys, all over the fingerboard. Since you can now play harmonic minor scales with two different fingerings, all you have to do is move them up to other frets in order to change keys. For example, you can play a *D* harmonic minor scale starting at the 5th fret on the fifth string as shown in the previous example. You can also play a *D* harmonic minor scale starting at the 10th fret on the sixth string using the Form 1 Minor fingering.

The following exercise patterns should be practiced in all keys. This will help to ensure your familiarity with the fingerings.

Play the above patterns by switching fingerings; for example, play the *D* harmonic minor pattern using the Form 1 Minor fingering, starting at the 10th fret on the sixth string, etc.

Next month we will continue with more fingerings for the harmonic minor scales. Till then, "straight ahead."

Arnie Berle's
FRETBOARD BASICS

Harmonic Minor Scale Fingerings, II

LAST MONTH WE LEARNED TWO FINGERINGS FOR the harmonic minor scale. Both started with the 2nd finger. We labeled them Form 1 Minor (with its tonic on the sixth string), and Form 2 Minor (with its tonic note on the fifth). Below are diagrams of both fingerings for review:

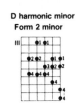

The next harmonic minor scale fingering will be referred to as the Form 3 Minor, and its tonic note occurs on the sixth string. This time, though, we will start with the 4th finger. Once again we will use the *A* harmonic minor scale as our example:

We will call our next harmonic minor scale fingering Form 4 Minor; it will start with the 4th finger on the fifth string (5th fret). We'll use the *D* harmonic minor scale for our example. Notice that this fingering does not allow for coverage of two complete octaves.

Here are the diagrams illustrating the Form 3 Minor and Form 4 Minor scale fingerings:

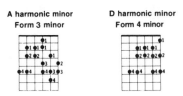

The following exercises are based on the Form 3 and Form 4 Minor scale fingerings. Play both exercises in all the harmonic minor keys, all over the fingerboard.

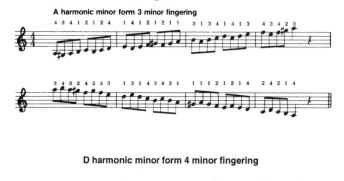

At this point you should be able to play four different fingerings for the harmonic minor scales, two beginning with the 2nd finger and two beginning with the 4th. Next month we'll learn how to play two more, starting with the 1st finger. Till then, "straight ahead."

Arnie Berle's
FRETBOARD BASICS

Harmonic Minor Scales, Part III

FOR THE PAST TWO MONTHS WE HAVE BEEN DISCUSS-ing the fingerings for the harmonic minor scales. We learned two that start with the 2nd finger and two that start with the 4th finger. This month we'll learn two more that begin with the 1st finger. This will give us a total of six different fingerings which will then enable us to play a harmonic minor scale anywhere on the fretboard.

Let's review the first four fingerings so that we can get a clearer picture of the two newest ones. The following diagrams illustrate two patterns for harmonic minor scales beginning with the 2nd finger:

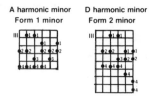

The diagrams below illustrate the harmonic minor scales that begin with the 4th finger:

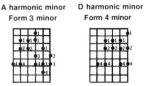

This next fingering for the harmonic minor scale we'll call the Form 5 minor; like Form 1 minor and Form 3 minor, its tonic note is located on the sixth string. This time, though, we will start with the 1st finger. We'll use the A harmonic minor scale for our example:

We'll call the next harmonic minor scale pattern Form 6 minor; it starts with the 1st finger on the fifth string. Here we will use the D harmonic minor scale for our example:

Let's look at two diagrams that illustrate the Form 5 minor and Form 6 minor scale fingerings:

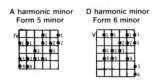

Both scale fingerings should be practiced in all the different harmonic minor keys up and down the fingerboard. After learning this month's forms we can now play in six different minor keys in any position. For example, in the fifth position we can play either the A minor or the D minor scales starting with the 2nd finger at the 5th fret. We can also play the B minor or E minor scales by starting with the 4th finger at the 7th fret. And with the 1st finger at the 3rd fret we can play the G minor or C minor scales. Besides playing six different harmonic minor scales in any single position, we can play any harmonic minor scale in six different locations on the fingerboard.

To ensure that you know the Form 5 minor and Form 6 minor fingerings really well, play the following exercises all over the fingerboard in all the different harmonic minor keys. Note the alternate fingerings shown in parentheses.

Next month we'll discuss the jazz minor scale. Until then, "straight ahead!"

28

Arnie Berle's
FRETBOARD BASICS

October 1980

Jazz Minor Scales, Part I

FOR THE PAST SEVERAL MONTHS WE'VE BEEN WORK-
ing with various harmonic minor scale fingerings, so now we will
delve into the jazz minor scale, which is derived from the more
traditional melodic minor scale. Before we get into the construction
of the jazz minor scale, though, let's review the melodic minor.

Below is the A melodic minor scale. Notice that it's formed by
raising the 6th and 7th tones of the natural minor scale as it ascends;
as it descends, though, the 6th and 7th tones are returned to their
original pitches:

A jazz minor scale is simply a natural minor scale with its 6th and
7th steps raised, both ascending *and* descending:

Another way of conceptualizing the jazz minor scale is to lower the
3rd step of any major scale. For example, to play an A jazz minor
scale, just lower the 3rd step, C♯ to C♮:

While this approach to the jazz minor offers a definite advantage
(since it is based on familiar major scale fingerings), there might be
some confusion about the correct key signature. For example, you
must not think that the key signature of the A jazz minor scale has
three sharps (as does the A major scale). It should in fact have the key
signature of its *relative major* scale, C (that is, no sharps or flats in
the key signature). The accidentals (in this case, sharps) are added
in the body of the music, rather than as a part of the key signature.
If you don't know what the relative major of the key is, count up a
minor 3rd (three half-steps, or three frets) from the tonic of your
minor key; this gives you the tonic of the relative major.

Since the jazz minor scales play such a large part in improvisation,
it is well worth the time to give them considerable attention and to
work on their fingerings so that you are completely at ease with
them. Let's take a look at some of these fingerings. Note that I will
stick with the traditionally accepted key signatures, although you
may view the scales in any manner you wish.

As with the scales we studied in previous months, we will use an
arbitrary method of identifying the fingerings. Any scale that has its
tonic note on the sixth string, and begins with the 2nd finger, we will
call the Form 1 jazz minor:

We'll use the D jazz minor scale that starts at the 5th fret of the fifth
string to illustrate the Form 2 *jazz* minor fingering:

The following fingerboard diagrams illustrate the fingerings for the
Form 1 jazz minor and Form 2 jazz minor scales:

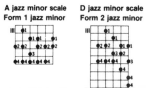

Both fingerings should be practiced in all minor keys up and down
the fretboard.

The following exercise patterns are given in order to ensure your
familiarity with the fingerings. Again, the patterns should be practiced in all keys.

Next month we'll continue with more fingerings for the jazz minor
scale. Till then, "straight ahead."

29

Arnie Berle's
FRETBOARD BASICS

November 1980

Jazz Minor Scale, Part II

LAST MONTH WE LEARNED TWO FINGERINGS FOR the very useful jazz minor scale. Both started with the 2nd finger. We labeled the first one Form 1 jazz minor; it starts on the sixth string. We named the second one Form 2 jazz minor; it starts on the fifth string. Here are diagrams of both:

We'll call the next fingering in our series Form 3 jazz minor. Like the Form 1 jazz minor, its tonic note lies on the sixth string, but this time the scale is initiated with the 4th finger. Below is the *A* jazz minor scale:

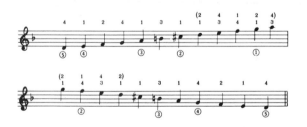

The next fingering that we encounter will be called the Form 4 jazz minor. It begins with the 4th finger on the fifth string. Notice that it doesn't allow for a full two-octave scale. Note, also, that there is an optional fingering to this scale form (shown in parentheses above the regular fingerings).

Here are three diagrams illustrating the Form 3 and Form 4 jazz minor scales, as well as the optional fingering for Form 4 jazz minor:

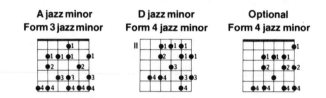

The following exercise patterns will help to ensure your familiarity with the fingerings of these scales. Play them in every key, all over the fingerboard.

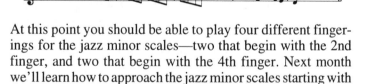

At this point you should be able to play four different fingerings for the jazz minor scales—two that begin with the 2nd finger, and two that begin with the 4th finger. Next month we'll learn how to approach the jazz minor scales starting with the 1st finger. Till then, "straight ahead."

Arnie Berle's
FRETBOARD BASICS

December 1980

Jazz Minor Scales, Part III

FOR THE PAST TWO MONTHS WE HAVE BEEN DIS-cussing jazz minor scale fingerings. Because this scale is used so much in jazz guitar soloing, I hope you're really practicing the material I've already given you. Before forging ahead right away, let's review the jazz minor scales discussed so far.

The following fretboard diagrams illustrate the fingerings for the jazz minor scales beginning with the 2nd finger, starting on the sixth and fifth strings, respectively.

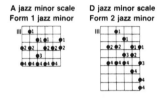

These next two diagrams illustrate the fingerings for the scales that begin with the 4th finger:

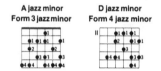

Now we're ready to move on to a new fingering for the jazz minor scale, which we'll call the Form 5 jazz minor. Its tonic note is located on the sixth string, and begins with the 1st finger. Once again, we'll use the *A* jazz minor scale for our example:

Our final fingering for the jazz minor scale we'll call the Form 6 jazz minor; its tonic note is on the fifth string. Always start this scale with the 1st finger. Our example uses the *D* jazz minor scale.

Here are two fretboard diagrams illustrating the Form 5 and Form 6 jazz minor scale fingerings:

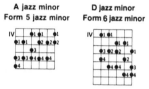

Both the Form 5 and Form 6 jazz minor scale fingerings should be practiced in every key all over the fingerboard.

At this point you can now play any jazz minor scale in six different positions on the fingerboard. (The application of these jazz minor scales will be covered in future columns.)

The following exercise patterns are designed to help ensure your familiarity with the Form 5 and Form 6 jazz minor scale fingerings. Play each pattern in different positions on the fingerboard. Till next month, keep practicing, and remember: straight ahead.

Arnie Berle's
FRETBOARD BASICS

Developing Jazz Feeling

IT'S HARD TO BELIEVE BUT WE'RE INTO ANOTHER NEW YEAR, so I thought I would respond to some of the mail I've gotten over the past year. To begin with, I must say a great big thanks to the people who have taken the time to write. As they know, I have tried to answer as many letters as I can. Many are from people who want to say thanks for what they have gotten out of the columns, while others are from guitarists who tell me that something in a column has cleared up a particular problem that has bothered them for years. As a teacher, I find these correspondences most gratifying.

One of the areas that seems to be of great interest to the majority of readers is scales and modes. Of course, much of this interest began in the late '50s because of the work of tenor saxophonist John Coltrane and those who followed him. There is now an abundance of new books on scales of all kinds being marketed. No matter which book a student buys, though, you must realize that these scales and modes are not the answer for someone who can't create a pretty or interesting melody out of a simple major scale. You cannot *get feeling* out of any book. Listen to records by trumpeter Louis Armstrong or Bix Beiderbecke to hear what feeling is all about. Listen to saxophonist Lester Young or guitarist Charlie Christian to hear what jazz is all about.

Just knowing all the modes, jazz minor scales, diminished scales, and the more exotic scales will not make you a jazz musician; they are only devices. Just being able to play them inside and out isn't enough, either. Some students can come up with great examples of improvisation based on this knowledge, while others just play exercises and show no feeling for jazz at all.

One of the best aids for developing a feel is to take a batch of solos by some of the great jazz musicians and try to sing them as close as possible to the original. Try to breathe where the soloist breathes, try to phrase exactly as he phrases, and then try to play the solo on your guitar, getting as close as possible to the original. After doing this for a dozen or more solos over the course of a year, you may begin to feel as the jazz musician feels. Hopefully some sort of transference takes place. Pianist Lennie Tristano did this with all of his pupils, and it does help. When you have developed some feel for what jazz is all about, then the knowledge of scales of all kinds will be a big help, especially if you're playing with bands using compositions based on modes or if you're given progressions with some greatly altered and extended chords. But remember, the feeling must be there.

Now let's suppose you do have a natural feeling for jazz or that you've acquired one through the process I've just outlined, and you can play some nice, interesting lines over the standard tunes in the jazz guitarist's repertoire. The next step is to see how you might make your improvised lines even more colorful and interesting. You are now at the point where musicians were in the late '30s and early '40s. At that time people like Charlie Parker, pianist Thelonius Monk, and trumpeter Dizzy Gillespie were experimenting with chords in hopes that they could create more interest in their solos. The great Charlie Christian was also there in New York at the time, and he, too, was contributing to this new approach to improvisation. They all met at Minton's club on 118th Street and Broadway, and exchanged ideas. This is how the bebop movement came into being.

What they were doing was simply extending and altering the chords of the jazz standards, tunes like "All The Things You Are," "Whispering," "Honeysuckle Rose," "How High The Moon," and others. The chord most suited for this extending and altering process was the dominant 7th. Below is a *G7* chord with the notes written as an arpeggio. Alongside of it is the extended version of the *G7*. Notice the addition of the 9th, 11th, and 13th:

Besides extending the chord these musicians also altered certain notes within the chord. For example, they could raise or flat the 5th and 9th, or try any combination of altered notes. Here are some altered and extended versions of the *G7*:

By altering and extending these dominant chords, the jazz players now had more notes to improvise with, and their solos became more colorful and interesting. These new notes created more tension, which was finally resolved when the players went to the tonic chord. Then musicians began realizing that it would be easier to think of certain scales that would contain the same notes as the chords that have been extended and altered. This would save having to learn which notes to alter or add. The scale that created the greatest number of altered notes is the melodic minor scale (ascending), which I call the jazz minor scale. For any unaltered dominant 7th chord, use the melodic minor scale built a half-step higher than the root of the dominant 7th, as illustrated below in the use of the *A♭* melodic minor scale for the *G7*:

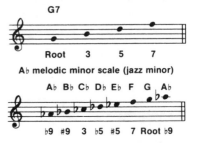

Notice that the number under each note of the scale indicates its relationship to the *G7* chord.

Next month I'll continue with more on the scales that are used to add color to an improvised solo. Until then, "straight ahead."

Arnie Berle's
FRETBOARD BASICS

Jazz Scales And Picking Patterns

LAST MONTH I WROTE ABOUT A VERY USEFUL scale that can be played against a dominant 7th chord and will produce many of the colorful and interesting notes that you hear great jazz musicians use. The scale is the ascending version of the melodic minor scale, which for our purposes we will refer to as the jazz minor scale. For any dominant 7th chord, use the jazz minor scale whose tonic or key note is a half-step higher than the root of the dominant 7th chord. So for a G7 chord, you use the Ab jazz minor scale. This Ab jazz minor scale will provide all of the colorful altered notes of the G7 chord such as the b5th, #5th, b9th, and #9th. Another example would be to use the F jazz minor scale for an E7 chord. For a series of good fingerings for the jazz minor scales, see my October through December '80 columns.

Often readers ask me about scales with such intriguing names as the super locrian or the lydian b7. These scales are simply modes derived from the jazz minor scale in the same way that the dorian or mixolydian modes come out of the major scale (for more on this, see my April through July '79 columns). The super locrian scale is the mode built from the 7th note of the jazz minor scale, so the G super locrian scale would be built from the 7th note of the Ab jazz minor scale. Since it comes from and contains the same notes as the Ab jazz minor scale, the G super locrian can be used against a G7 chord. The lydian b7 scale is a mode derived from the fourth note of the jazz minor scale. For example, the Db lydian b7 scale is built from the fourth note of the Ab jazz minor scale. It follows once again that the Db lydian b7 scale may also be used to improvise against the G7 chord. The point of all this is to show you that many of these scales with frightening names often contain the same notes, while starting from a different tonic note. Below are the three scales discussed above. Notice how all of them contain the same notes. I've included the letter names of the notes for nonreaders:

Although all three scales contain the same notes, many guitarists prefer using the Db lydian b7 scale against the G7, since it is only a half-step away from the C, its natural resolution. I suggest that you try to figure out the scales that can be used against other dominant 7th chords. We'll do more on improvising scales in future columns.

Other questions I am frequently asked concern ways of holding the pick and methods of picking. Recently I had an occasion to moderate a panel of five of the leading New York studio guitarists, and we got into this kind of a discussion. The general opinion was that many great guitarists keep some part of their right-hand fingers on the guitar as a reference point, while other equally great guitarists don't keep any part of their right hand on the guitar. You pay your money and take your pick. As far as how to alternate picking strokes, again the opinion was that it varies according to the way the music is going and where you want the accents. There are times when consecutive up-picks or consecutive down-picks work well. When notes are played on the same string, then alternate picking would be best. Given the same piece of music, ten different guitarists would most likely pick it differently. Below are two examples of picking the same melodic phrase:

I hope the above has been helpful. Keep the questions coming in because they help determine future columns. You can write to me care of *Guitar Player,* 20605 Lazaneo, Cupertino, CA 95014. Until next month, remember: "straight ahead."

Ab jazz minor

| Ab | Bb | Cb | Db | Eb | F | G | Ab |

Db lydian b7

| Db | Eb | F | G | Ab | Bb | Cb | Db |

G super locrian

| G | Ab | Bb | Cb | Db | Eb | F | G |

Arnie Berle's
FRETBOARD BASICS

March 1981

Arpeggiated Triads

FOR THE PAST SEVERAL MONTHS MY COLUMNS have all been based on various kinds of scales and their fingerings. The reaction from readers has been very good since many students don't have the benefit of a private teacher. Now, in response to many requests, I want to go into a study of arpeggio fingerings. For anyone interested in learning to improvise, the importance of knowing arpeggios all over the fingerboard cannot be stressed too much. Improvising often combines the use of scale tones and arpeggios. Some players stress more of one than the other, but overall most musicians use a good balance of both.

A jazz musician who tends to use more scale tones is often called a "linear" player, and one who tends to favor chord tones is called a "change" player. John Coltrane was an excellent saxophonist who at various times demonstrated both types of playing. In his famous recording of "Giant Steps," for example, he leaned toward playing right on the chord tones. On other recordings, such as "My Favorite Things" [both cuts on *Best Of John Coltrane,* Atlantic. 1541], he tended to play more scalar. One writer, in fact, described John as having "sheets of sound" because he played up and down scales with so many notes. Coltrane himself explained, "I had to get all the notes of the scale."

Let's begin with an explanation of what an arpeggio is. It is simply the playing of the notes in a chord one at a time rather than all at once. This example shows an arpeggiated *C* chord:

The chord shown above is known as a triad, which is just another way of saying a three-note chord. It does not have a 7th added to it. Although 7th chords are in the basic vocabulary of jazz, I'd like to start this series with triads, and from there we'll go on to the 7th, 9th, 11th, and 13th chord arpeggios.

Now let's see where arpeggios come from. In this case, they are just the notes of a triad played singly. All triads come from scales. The major triad is derived from the first, third, and fifth notes of the major scale:

The four different quality chords used in jazz are the major, minor, augmented, and diminished chords. The minor chord is formed from the first, third, and fifth notes of the *minor* scale:

The augmented chord is formed from the first, third, and fifth notes of the *whole-tone* scale:

And the diminished chord is built from the first, third, and fifth notes of the *diminished* scale:

A simpler way at arriving at the various triad qualities is to follow an easy mathematical formula and form all triads from the basic major triad. For the minor triad, just flat the third note of the major triad. The augmented triad raises the fifth note of the major triad, and the diminished triad flats the third and fifth notes of the major triad:

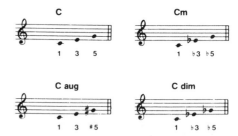

Next month we will start playing these triads all over the fingerboard, using different fingerings. Until then it would be good to practice writing out the four triad qualities in every key. Until next month, remember: straight ahead.

Arnie Berle's
FRETBOARD BASICS

April 1981

Chord Arpeggios

LAST MONTH WE DISCUSSED WAYS OF CONSTRUCT-ing the major, minor, augmented and diminished chords. For the next several columns, we will go into the various fingering possibilities for arpeggiating these different chords. First of all, let me explain that an arpeggio is simply the playing of the notes of a chord singly—one note at a time—rather than simultaneously. Mastery of this technique is essential for anyone who wants to improvise, since improvisation is the creation of melodies based on the notes in a given series of chords.

Before we go into the fingerings, let's review how these chords are formed. In general, all chords are formed by taking the first, third, and fifth notes of any scale. Therefore, if we take the first, third, and fifth notes of the major, minor, whole-tone, or diminished scales, we form the major, minor, augmented, and diminished chords. You can see how important it is to know your scales. If you are unsure of your scale fingerings, go back to my columns starting with the November '79 issue.

Improvisation is based on scale tones as well as chord tones. Now, it is still possible to form these various chords if you at least know the major chord fingering, because then all you have to do is just alter certain notes of the major chord. For now, let's just work on the major and minor chord arpeggios based on the sixth [low E] and fifth strings, beginning with the 2nd finger:

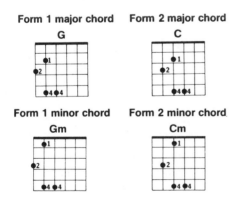

Notice that to change a major chord to a minor chord, just lower the 3rd of the major chord. Below is the written notation for the arpeggios just given:

The following exercise is based on the major-chord arpeggios whose roots are on the sixth string. We can call this the major chord fingering Form 1, since it is derived from the Form 1 scale fingering (for more on this, see my November '79 column). The Roman numerals indicate the position:

This exercise is based on the major chord arpeggios whose roots are on the fifth string. We can call this fingering the major chord fingering Form 2, since it is derived from the major scale fingering Form 2:

The following exercise shows how to play through the cycle of fifths by using both Form 1 and Form 2 major chord fingerings:

Now repeat all of the previous exercises, but convert the major chords to minor chords by lowering the 3rds (see chord arpeggio fingerings). Next month, we'll go on with more fingers for the chord arpeggios. Until then, remember: straight ahead.

35

More Chord Arpeggios

LAST MONTH WE STARTED OUR STUDY OF VARIOUS fingerings for chord arpeggios. We began with the major and minor arpeggios that had their roots on the 6th and 5th strings and were played beginning with the 2nd finger. Now let's play the same arpeggios off the same strings, but this time we will start with our 4th finger. The diagrams below show the fingerings for the *Amaj* chord arpeggio. We will call this the Form 3 major chord arpeggio fingering because it is derived from our Form 3 major scale fingering (for more on this, see my January '80 column). The *Am* chord arpeggio is formed by flatting the 3rd of the major chord:

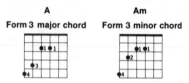

Below is the written notation for the major and minor chord arpeggios:

The following exercise is based on the major chord arpeggios in Form 3. Remember that the root of each chord is played on the 6th string. The Roman numerals indicate the position:

Repeat the same exercise, this time playing all chords as minors by flatting the 3rd of each, as shown in the diagrams.

Now let's play the major and minor chord arpeggios whose roots are on the 5th string. We will call these Form 4 apreggio fingerings because they are derived from the Form 4 major scale positions shown in my January '80 column. Below are diagrams that illustrate the fingerings:

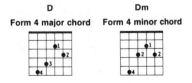

This is the musical notation for the Form 4 major and minor chord arpeggios as shown in the diagrams:

The following exercise is based on Form 4 major chord arpeggios played up the fingerboard. Remember that the root of each chord is played on the 5th string.

Repeat the above exercise, playing each chord as a minor by flatting the 3rd.

By using the Forms 1 and 2 chord arpeggios learned last month and this month's Forms 3 and 4, it's possible to play all of the major chords with a minimum amount of movement. See the exercise below:

Once again, for additional practice, repeat the exercise playing all chords as minors. See the chord diagrams for the correct fingerings.

Next month we'll learn still more fingerings for the major and minor chord arpeggios. Till then, "straight ahead!"

36

Arnie Berle's
FRETBOARD BASICS

June 1981

More Chord Arpeggios

IN MY LAST TWO COLUMNS I SHOWED HOW TO PLAY minor and major chord arpeggios off the sixth and fifth strings, starting with the 2nd and 4th fingers. Now we will play the major and minor arpeggios whose roots are on the sixth and fifth strings, but this time starting with the 1st finger. The diagrams below show the fingering for the *Fmaj chord* arpeggio, which we will call the form 5 because it is derived from the form 5 major scale fingering (see my March '80 column for more on this). The *Fm* chord apreggio is also shown, formed by flatting the 3rd of the major chord:

Here is the musical notation for the major and minor arpeggios. Play each arpeggio up the fingerboard, and remember that the root is the note played on the sixth string with the 1st finger:

Now let's play the major and minor arpeggios whose roots are on the fifth string. We'll call these the form 6 major or minor arpeggios fingerings, derived from the form 6 major scale fingerings shown in the March '80 column. The diagrams below illustrate them. It's important to understand that the *arpeggio* fingerings are always derived from the *scale* fingerings from which the chords come. Occasionally there are some alternates, but these are usually for convenience.

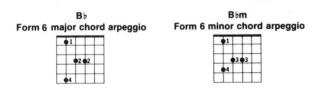

Below is the musical notation for the chord diagrams. Play each arpeggio up the fingerboard and remember that the root of each chord is the note played with the 1st finger on the fifth string:

The following study is based on all of the major chords, using a minimum amount of movement. This is made possible by using all of the arpeggio fingerings from the past three columns. In other words, by using forms 1 through 6, you can play through all of the

major chord arpeggios. I have indicated the form over the chord symbol. Try as many combinations of forms as you can, starting on different parts of the fingerboard.

By flatting the 3rd note of the major chord apreggio, we form the minor arpeggio. This exercise is based on the minor arpeggios in the same manner that you just played through the major ones:

The following sequences are based on the major and minor arpeggios played as triplets:

We'll go on with our study of arpeggios next month. Until then, remember: Straight ahead!

Seventh Chords

IN THE LAST THREE COLUMNS WE HAVE DISCUSSED the fingerings for the major and minor chords containing only three different tones. These are called triads and are derived from the major and minor scales by taking the first, third, and fifth tones. Now I want to show you the fingerings for major 7th, minor 7th, and dominant 7th chords, since these are important to any study of improvisation. Once again I must remind you that all chords are derived from scales, so before we get into the various fingerings, let's see how these chords are formed.

The major 7th chord is formed by taking the first, third, fifth, and seventh notes from the major scale:

It is very important that you understand the next concept: All major scales have within themselves six additional scales called *modes*. For example, if we start on the second note of any major scale and play up the scale to its octave, we have another scale that is known as the dorian mode. If we start on the third note of any major scale and play up to its octave, we have a scale called the phrygian mode. This process is continued with all the rest of the notes of the major scale, and in this way we have all the modes contained within the major scale. The key signature of each mode is the same as the major scale from which the mode is derived.

By taking the first, third, fifth, and seventh notes of each mode we form the chord that is associated with that particular mode. For example, by taking these four notes of the *D* dorian mode, which is the mode built from the second note of the *C* major scale, we form the *Dm7* chord. The *D* dorian mode is then the improvising scale for that *Dm7* chord. Below is an example of modes taken from the *C* major scale plus the chord formed from each mode:

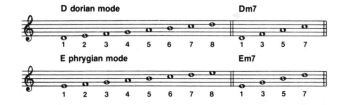

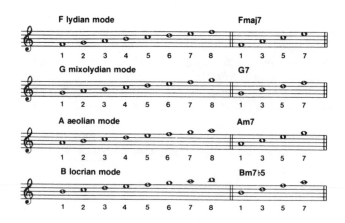

Now that we have formed all of the chords that can be derived from the *C* major scale and its related modal scales, let's place all of the chords over each note of the original *C* major scale:

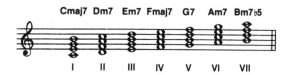

The Roman numerals under each chord indicate its relative position within the major scale.

In past columns we have learned that the most important of all the chords are the I, II, and V. We also learned in past columns how to play the very important II-V-I progression all over the fingerboard. In the next series of columns you will be given arpeggio fingerings for these same chords played all over the fingerboard. Until then, "Straight ahead."

Arnie Berle's
FRETBOARD BASICS

Fingering II-V-I Chords

IN LAST MONTH'S COLUMN WE LEARNED THAT WITHIN every major scale there are six additional scales called modes. We further learned that by taking the first, third, fifth, and seventh notes from the major scale and the modes contained within, we can form all of the chords that are relative to that major scale. In other words, we can form all of the chords that may be used to harmonize a melody based on that particular scale. This next series of columns will show you the fingerings for the very important II-V-I chords, which are the basis for much jazz improvisation.

Let's first look at the major 7th chord, which is the I chord in every major scale. Below is the fingering for the major scale that has its tonic note on the sixth string. In past columns I have labeled this fingering Form 1:

The fingering for the major 7th arpeggio is derived from the fingerings of the major scale shown above. We can call this the major 7th chord fingering Form 1 since it is derived from the major scale fingering Form 1. Notice that the open circled note indicates the position of added tones in the lower register:

Very often the I chord is played as a major 6th. That fingering is shown below. Also, the major 9th is often added to the major 7th chord. That, too, is illustrated below. Notice that all chord fingerings are taken from the major scale fingering Form 1:

The above arpeggios should be practiced up the fingerboard. Remember that they are based on the Form 1 major scales whose tonic notes are on the sixth string beginning with the 2nd finger.

The V chord in the major scale is formed by taking the first, third, fifth, and seventh notes of the mixolydian mode (for more on this, see my July '81 column). The chord is called the dominant 7th, and the mixolydian mode is also called the dominant 7th scale. Below is

a diagram of the D mixolydian mode whose tonic is on the fifth string. This can also be called the D dominant 7th scale. Notice that the fingering is derived from the G major scale Form 1. The D7 chord arpeggio is also given:

The dominant 7th chord may be extended to the 9th and 13th:

The II chord in the major scale is formed by taking the first, third, fifth, and seventh notes from the dorian mode. The chord is called the minor 7th, and the dorian mode is also called the minor 7th scale. Below is a diagram of the A dorian mode with its tonic on the sixth string. It is also called the A minor 7th scale. Notice that the fingering is once again derived from the G major scale Form 1. The Am7 chord arpeggio is also shown:

The minor 7th chord may be extended to the 9th:

Next month I'll give you some exercises to ensure that you know the various arpeggios all over the fingerboard. In the meantime, play each arpeggio up the fingerboard. Till next month, "straight ahead."

39

Arnie Berle's
FRETBOARD BASICS

September 1981

Fingering II-V-I Chords

PROBABLY THE MOST DIFFICULT PROBLEM FOR THE student studying improvisation on guitar is learning to locate all the notes he hears in his head on the fingerboard. This series of columns is designed to help you develop some system of fingerings that will cover the whole fingerboard. So far we have used the II-V-I chords, which are most often found in compositions favored by jazz players. This month let's study more examples of what might be done on each of these three chords using major scale Form 1 fingerings.

Here is an exercise based on the I (major 7th) chord played up the fingerboard starting with the *Gmaj7* arpeggio played at the 3rd fret, sixth string:

Just using the notes of the *Gmaj7,* here are some examples of patterns or licks. Be sure that you can play each example up the fingerboard, just as you did in the exercise above:

In the examples below, the 6th and 9th are added to increase the melodic possibilities. Again, play each example up the fingerboard, and see last month's column for the *G6* and *Gmaj9* chord arpeggios:

The Am7 (II) chord in the key of *G* played up the fingerboard is shown below. The fingerings are taken from the Form 1 scale fingerings:

These patterns are based on the notes of the *Am7* chord. Notice that measure 3 has the added 9th and measure 4 has the added 6th and 9th. Play each pattern up the fingerboard:

Below is a series of dominant 7th chords played up the fingerboard starting with the *D7,* the V chord in the key of *G:*

The following patterns are based on the *D7* chord. Again, for greater melodic possibilities we will extend the chord to the 9th and the 13th:

Next month we'll learn a whole new set of fingerings for the same II-V-I chords. Till then, remember: "straight ahead."

Arnie Berle's
FRETBOARD BASICS

October 1981

Form 2 Arpeggio Fingerings

IN THE PAST TWO COLUMNS I GAVE YOU THE FINGER-ings for the II-V-I chords derived from the major scale that used Form 1 fingerings. This month we will work with another set of fingerings for the same chords, but this time they will be taken from the major scale that uses Form 2 fingerings. You must understand that the reason for learning these various fingerings for these often-used chords is so that you can play a chord arpeggio from anyplace on the fingerboard. The more fingerings you have at your command, the more freedom you will have in playing all over the fingerboard.

Below is the fingering that I gave in previous columns and which I arbitrarily labeled Form 2 major scale fingerings. All of our chord arpeggio fingerings will be derived from this, so learn it well and play it up the frets. The open circles indicate notes that are within the scale, but are below the tonic note.

The fingering for the arpeggio of the I chord or the major 7th chord is derived from the fingering of the major scale shown above. Notice that in order to play all of the notes contained in the chord, we will have to go below the root of the chord, so we will go down to the notes that are available to use on the sixth string:

Very often the I chord may be played as a major 6th or a major 9th chord. The fingerings for these arpeggios are shown below:

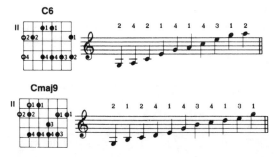

Remember that all of the above chords have their root played on the fifth string. Play all arpeggios up the fingerboard.

The II chord in the major scale is a minor 7th derived from the dorian mode. For more on this, see my July '81 column. The dorian mode may also be thought of as the minor 7th scale. Below is the D dorian mode or D minor 7th scale, and alongside is the Dm7 chord arpeggio.

Notice that the fingerings are all derived from our original C major scale Form 2:

The minor 7th chord may be extended to a 9th chord. Below is the Dm9th chord arpeggio fingering:

The V chord in the major scale is derived from the mixolydian mode, as I explained in my July '81 column. This is called the dominant 7th chord, and the mixolydian mode is also called the dominant 7th scale. The following diagrams illustrate the scale and the chord arpeggio, and all fingerings are derived from the Form 2 major scale fingerings. Notice the alteration in the fingering of the G7 arpeggio:

The dominant 7th chord may be extended to a 9th chord and a 13th chord, and their arpeggios are:

Remember that the 9th is the same note as the 2nd, and the 13th is the same as the 6th. This is why those notes are included in all of the above arpeggio diagrams. Next month we'll play some exercises based on the above arpeggios. Until then, "straight ahead."

41

Seventh Chord Arpeggio Fingerings

IN LAST MONTH'S COLUMN WE LEARNED THE PATTERNS for the II-V-I chord arpeggios based on the Form 2 major scale fingerings. The designation Form 2 is simply an arbitrary labeling of a particular shape for the major scale, as opposed to other fingerings for the major scales which I have designated by other labels, such as Form 1 or Form 3. This month, let's continue our study of Form 2 major scale patterns for II-V-I chord arpeggios.

Here is an exercise based on the I chord—or the major 7th chord—played up the fingerboard starting with the *Cmaj7* chord on the 3rd fret of the fifth string:

When improvising, guitarists rarely just play up the notes of a chord in the manner that you just did. The purpose in working through the above exercise is to acquaint you with the notes and fingerings for each major 7th arpeggio. You should be able to improvise or play around on the notes of the arpeggio, so the following patterns are examples of what might be done using only the notes of the major 7th. Play each example up the fingerboard just as you did with the above exercise. Some of the examples use notes of the chord that are located on the sixth string. This works perfectly, since it gives you more notes to choose from:

In the following examples the 6th and 9th are added to the major 7th, increasing the melodic possibilities. See last month's column for the *C6* and *Cmaj9* arpeggios:

This exercise is based on the IIm7 chords derived from the Form 2 scale fingerings. The exercise begins with the *Dm7*—the II chord in the key of *C*. It then continues up the fingerboard:

The following patterns are based on only the notes of the *Dm7* arpeggio. Play each example up the fretboard:

Adding the 6th and the 9th to the chord increases the melodic possibilities:

The exercise below is based on the V7 chords played up the fingerboard. The first chord is *G7,* which is the V chord in the key of *C*. Notice that for the root we can dip down to the sixth string which gives us a greater range of notes:

The following patterns are based only on the notes of the *G7* chord. Play each pattern up the fingerboard:

Here the 6th and 9th are added:

Next month we'll learn another set of fingerings for the II-V-I chord arpeggios. Till then, "straight ahead."

Arnie Berle's
FRETBOARD BASICS

December 1981

Common Jazz Scale Fingerings

THIS MONTH WE WILL CONTINUE TO LEARN THE DIF-ferent fingerings that are possible for the major, minor, and dominant 7th chord arpeggios. All of the shapes in this column series are derived from the various major scale patterns. So far we have worked with arpeggios derived from major scale Forms 1 and 2, and now we will look at those from Form 3 major scale fingerings, which are commonly used by many jazz musicians because they allow you to play in any major key whose tonic note is on the sixth string. This gives you two full octaves to play in. Learning these new patterns will increase your ability to play in more areas of the fingerboard, while decreasing your need to jump around.

Below is the Form 3 major scale pattern. Play it up the fingerboard. All of our arpeggios will be taken from this scale. Notice the two possible fingerings for the seventh note of the scale in the lower octave. The choice of which fingering to use depends on the notes that come before or after that note. The open circled notes are also within the key, but they are below the tonic note:

The fingering for the I chord arpeggio (or the major 7th arpeggio) is shown below. In order to make full use of all the notes contained in the chord, we can use those notes that are below the root. Again, all arpeggios should be played up the fingerboard:

You can also add the 9th of the chord to the major 7th. The I chord may also be played as a major 6th chord. Here are the patterns for both:

The II chord in the major scale is a minor 7th derived from the dorian mode (see my July '81 column). The mode is the scale that is applied to the minor 7th chord when improvising. There are other scales, too, which will be discussed at a later time. The dorian mode may also be thought of as the minor 7th scale. Below is the B dorian or B minor 7th scale and the Bm7 chord arpeggio. The fingerings are all derived

from our original Form 3 A major scale. The notes below and above the tonic notes of the scale are circled:

The minor 7th chord may be extended to a 9th chord. Below is the Bm9 chord arpeggio pattern:

The V chord in the major scale comes from the mixolydian mode (once again, see my July '81 column for more information). This is called the dominant 7th chord, and the mixolydian mode may be called the dominant 7th scale. These diagrams illustrate the E mixolydian or E7th scale, and the E7 chord arpeggio is derived from it. Again, the fingerings are from the Form 3 major scale:

The dominant 7th chord may be extended to a 9th and 13th chord:

Next month we'll play some exercises based on the arpeggios you've just learned. Until then, "straight ahead."

43

Arnie Berle's
FRETBOARD BASICS

January 1982

Alternate Patterns And Exotic Scales

ONCE AGAIN WE'RE INTO A NEW YEAR, SO THOUGHT I'D take some time out from my series of columns on chord arpeggios to answer some of the mail I've gotten recently. First of all, I'd like to wish all of the readers a happy New Year and thank those who have written me kind words and compliments (mail can be sent to me either in care of *Guitar Player,* or to my studio at 87 Candlewood Dr., Yonkers, NY 10710). I am happy to receive the amount of mail that I get, and all of the columns I write are in response to readers' requests. Regretfully, I can't always answer each letter, but I try to address as many as I can in the columns.

Here's a question that I'm frequently asked: "Must I learn all of the scale patterns and all of the different arpeggio fingerings that have been given in your columns recently?" Fingerings for both scales and arpeggios are given because so many readers have asked for them. It's true, of course, that many great players have been very successful without knowing all of the different fingerings I have presented, but that's no reason to limit yourself. The more ways you can play a particular scale or arpeggio, the less you will have to jump around the fingerboard to find the patterns you are accustomed to playing. No matter where you are on the guitar, you should be able to play any scale or arpeggio. Many great guitarists are not ashamed to admit that they constantly practice new fingerings, runs, or patterns in keys all over the fretboard.

Another question sometimes asked is about the alternate fingerings that are sometimes given in the scales or arpeggios: "How do you choose which fingering to use?" The alternate patterns are given to let you know that you have choices and that you need not to be so rigid. The choice depends on the note that comes before or after the note in question. You have to choose which fingering—the given or the alternate—will best lead you into the next note. In the final analysis, fingerings are subject to change according to the size of your hand and the situation you find yourself in.

Someone asked me if I could give the fingerings for the Japanese modes and the Hungarian Gypsy, Japanese, and Hindu scales. Okay, here they are, but you work out your own fingerings:

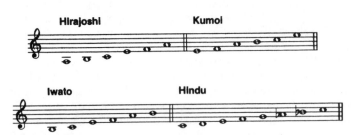

I'm giving these to you but can you play the blues with them or a nice chorus on the chords to "I Got Rhythm"? Many people want to learn exotic scales in hopes that it will make them a better player or to impress friends with their vast knowledge. Nothing wrong with increasing your knowledge or command of jazz vocabulary, but if you can't play something pretty using the conventional major and minor scales, then all of the scales in the Orient won't help. [*Ed. Note:* Guitar Player *published a study of over two dozen exotic scales in the August '80 issue.*]

Some readers have expressed curiosity about where the expression "straight ahead" comes from. When I was a student some years ago, it was a common parting expression that many musicians and music students used. It simply meant to put blinders on and not allow ourselves to be distracted from our studies of music and our goals, to just think "straight ahead."

Next month we'll return to the regular series of columns. When you're practicing and a friend calls to ask you to go out and play some ball, just remember: "straight ahead."

CHORD DIAGRAM LEGEND

In all *Guitar Player* chord diagrams, vertical lines represent the strings, and horizontal lines represent the frets. The following symbols are used:

— =nut; indicates 1st position   **X** = muted string or string not played

⌒ =bar (partial or full)   **O** = open string

• = placement of left-hand fingers

Roman numeral = fret at which chord is located

Arabic numeral = left-hand finger (e.g. 1 = index, etc.)

Arnie Berle's
FRETBOARD BASICS

February 1982

Major, Minor & Dominant Seventh Chords

LAST MONTH I INTERRUPTED MY REGULAR SERIES of columns on scale fingering possibilities and II V I chord arpeggio patterns to answer some questions readers sent in. Now it's time to continue where I left off in my study, so dig out your December '81 *Guitar Player* and review the Form 3 fingerings given in my column.

The following exercise, which is based on the major 7th (or I) chord arpeggio, shows the major 7th chords played up the fingerboard starting with the *A* major 7th whose root is on the 5th fret of the sixth string. The pattern is derived from the Form 3 scale fingering shown in the December column:

The above exercise is simply to help you locate some of the major 7th chords along the fingerboard. It's important to understand that no improvisation is based on the notes of the chord played as shown in the exercise. Keep in mind that while improvising, you normally wouldn't play straight up an arpeggio as in the above example.

While still containing only the notes of the chord, the following two patterns are more typical of what might be an improvisation on a major 7th chord. These examples are based on the *A* major 7th chord, but you should play the pattern up the fingerboard in other keys:

These next patterns include the 6th and major 9th, added notes that increase the melodic possibilities. See my December column for the *A6* and *Amaj9* arpeggios. Play each pattern up the fretboard:

The following exercise is based on the minor 7th (or II) arpeggios played up the neck. Again, these fingerings are derived from Form 3:

The patterns below are based on the *Bm7* chord. Notice that the last two make use of the 6th and 9th of the chord. Play each pattern up the fingerboard:

The following series of dominant 7th (or V) chords are also played up the fretboard. In order to make greater use of the available notes, this arpeggio differs from previous examples by starting on the 3rd rather than on the root of the chord:

These last patterns are based on the *E7* chord. The 9th and 13th are added to the basic chord tones. As you play each pattern up the fretboard, you should be able to name each note, as well as its numerical position in the chord:

Next month we'll learn another fingering for the II V I chord arpeggios. Until then, remember: "Straight ahead."

Arnie Berle's
FRETBOARD BASICS

Alternate Fingerings For Seventh Chords

So far, we've studied the fingerings for these various arpeggios based on Forms 1, 2, and 3 of the major scales.

Now we will learn to use arpeggio fingerings derived from the Form 4 major scale, the pattern of which is shown below. Notice that the tonic or key note starts on the fifth string. Play the scale pattern up the fingerboard and learn it well, since all of our arpeggios will be based on it. Notice that the scale is only playable for an octave and a half without going out of position. However, you can add to it by playing notes that are contained in the key and go down to the sixth string. The circled notes are within the key, but below the tonic note:

Below is the fingering for the major 7th chord arpeggio (the I chord). In order to make full use of all the notes available in the chord, we can use those notes that are below the root, going down to the sixth string. All arpeggios should be played up the fingerboard. Be sure that you can name each note and know its relationship to the chord, such as root, 3rd, 5th, and 7th:

The 9th may be added to the major 7th. The I chord may also be played as a major 6th chord. Both patterns are shown here:

The II chord in the major scale is a minor 7th derived from the dorian mode (see my July '81 column for more on modes). The mode is the scale that is applied to the II minor 7th chord when improvising.

The dorian mode may also be thought of as the minor 7th scale. Below is the E dorian mode or Em7 scale, as well as the Em7 chord arpeggio. The fingerings are derived from the Form 4 D major scale. Notes below the root are also used in the arpeggio:

The 9th may also be added to the minor 7th. Here is the Em9 chord arpeggio pattern:

The V chord in the major scale is derived from the mixolydian mode. This may be called the dominant 7th chord, and the mixolydian mode may be called the dominant 7th scale. These diagrams illustrate the A mixolydian mode or the A7 scale, as well as the A7 chord arpeggio derived from it:

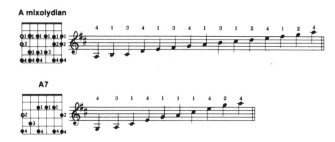

The dominant 7th chord may be extended to a 9th and 13th chord:

Notice that with all of the arpeggios I've included the notes that lie beneath the lowest root of the arpeggio. However, it would be good practice to play each arpeggio starting from the root so that you get to hear the chord sound from its root.

Next month we'll play some exercises based on the arpeggios you've just learned. Until then, "straight ahead."

Arnie Berle's
FRETBOARD BASICS

May 1982

Scale Fingerings For I, II, And V Chords

IF YOU HAVE BEEN REGULARLY FOLLOWING THIS COL-umn, you should by now have at your command at least four different possible fingerings for the major, minor, and dominant 7th chord arpeggios. The ability to play these arpeggios in any position on the fingerboard is important for any aspiring jazz guitarist. If you are limited in your ability to play these arpeggios, you will find yourself having to jump all over the fingerboard. By practicing the examples in this series of columns, you can have a fingering available to you in any area of the fretboard you find yourself.

Now we will consider still another set of fingerings for chord arpeggios. These will be based on what I call Form 5 scale finger-ings. Below is the Form 5 scale fingering pattern. The open circled notes indicate notes that are within the key but extend beyond the highest tonic note. Play the scale up the fingerboard:

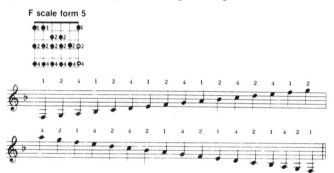

The pattern for the I—or major 7th—chord is given below. Play all of the arpeggios up the fingerboard. Notice the adjustment in the arpeggio fingering, which was done to make playing it easier and more practical:

The following diagrams illustrate the major 9th and major 6th chords, both of which may be played in place of the major 7th. (Both chords are considered I chords.) Play each arpeggio up the frets:

The II chord in the major scale is a minor 7th, and it is derived from the dorian mode, which I discussed in my July '81 column. This mode is the scale that is applied to the minor 7th chord when improvising. The dorian mode may also be thought of as the minor 7th scale. Below is the G dorian mode and the Gm7 chord arpeggio.

Remember that all of these examples are taken from the Form 5 pattern, and they should all be played up the neck:

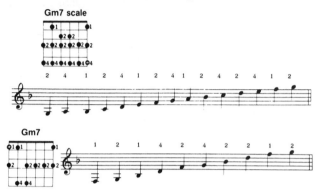

The minor 7th chord may be extended to a minor 9th chord:

The dominant 7th chord—also called the V chord—comes from the mixolydian mode (also termed the dominant 7th scale). The dia-grams that follow illustrate the C mixolydian mode or C7 dominant scale, as well as the C7 chord arpeggio. Open circled notes indicate notes above and below the upper and lower tonics of the scale:

The dominant 7th chord may be extended to 9th and 13th chords:

Next month we will play some exercises based on the above arpeggios. Till then, "straight ahead."

Arnie Berle's
FRETBOARD BASICS

June 1982

Variations In Arpeggio Fingerings

LAST MONTH WE LEARNED AN ALTERNATE SET OF fingerings for the major (I), minor (II), and dominant (V) 7th chord arpeggios. These were all based on what I call the Form 5 major scale fingering patterns. This month we'll play some exercises based on these chord arpeggios. These exercises are designed to help you learn various arpeggio fingerings in patterns other than those that just go straight up the chord tones. When you are improvising or reading music, it isn't often that you play the notes of an arpeggio in the order of root, 3rd, 5th, and 7th. The notes are most often played in a mixed order, so you must be able to locate any note in the chord and know what each finger is playing.

First, let's play the major 7th chord arpeggio in order (be sure to continue this and the rest of this column's musical examples up the fingerboard):

The next two exercises are based on the *Fmaj7* arpeggio, but the notes are mixed in an order similar to an improvisation:

These patterns are based on the major 6th and major 9th chords (see last month's column for fingerings for these arpeggios):

The following exercise is based on the minor 7th chord played up the fingerboard:

These patterns are based on the *Gm7* chord. Notice that the 9th is also added to the chord:

This is built from the dominant 7th or V chord:

This month's final patterns are based on the *C7* chord. Notice the addition of the 9th and 13th to the basic chord, as well as fingering adjustments that make the pattern easier to play:

Next month we'll learn our last set of fingerings for the major, minor, and dominant 7th chords. Till then, "straight ahead!"

Arnie Berle's
FRETBOARD BASICS

Major, Minor, And Dominant 7th Chord Fingerings

WELL, HERE WE ARE, DOWN TO OUR LAST SET OF FIN-gerings for the major, minor, and dominant 7th chord arpeggios. If you have been following this column regularly, you should have a total of six possible ways to finger these chord arpeggios. Knowing all these fingerings eliminates the need to jump all over the finger-board. By now you should be able to play in six different keys in any area of the fretboard.

Below is the Form 6 major scale fingering pattern. The open circled notes indicate those notes that are within the key but below the lowest tonic. Also notice the alternate fingering for the note played on the 1st fret, second string:

The pattern for the major 7th chord—the I chord—is given below. Notice the adjustment in the fingering for the arpeggio, which is done to make it less awkward:

The major 6th and major 9th chords may be played in place of the major 7th:

The II chord in the major scale is a minor 7th derived from the dorian mode (see my July '81 column for further information on modes). The mode is the scale that is applied to the IIm7 chord when improvising. The dorian mode may also be thought of as the m7 scale. Below is the C dorian mode and the Cm7 chord arpeggio. Be sure to observe the adjustments in the fingering for the arpeggio:

The 9th may also be added to the minor 7th chord. Here is the arpeggio:

The V7 chord is derived from the mixolydian mode. This mode may also be called the dominant 7th scale. The diagrams below illustrate the F mixolydian mode or the F7 scale and the F7 chord arpeggio:

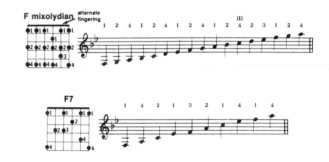

The dominant 7th chord may be extended to the 9th (G) and 13th (D):

Next month we'll have some exercises based on the arpeggios just learned. Until then, "straight ahead."

More Patterns, Less Fingerboard Movement

IN LAST MONTH'S COLUMN WE LEARNED OUR FINAL set of fingerings for the II-V-I chord arpeggios. Those patterns, as well as the ones given in this month's column, are taken from the Form 6 major scale fingerings. Now we'll play some exercises based on each of these chord arpeggios.

The music below is based on the Form 6 major 7th arpeggios played up the fingerboard starting with the *Bb maj7* chord whose root is on the 1st fret of the fifth string. Be sure to continue this exercise, as well as all those that follow, up the fingerboard as far as you can go:

These patterns are based on the notes of the *Bbmaj7* chord:

The next two examples are based on the major 6th and major 9th chords (see last month's column for the fingerings for the *Bb6* and *Bbmaj9* arpeggios):

This next exercise is based on the minor 7th chords played up the fingerboard. The minor 7th chord in this column series is considered the II chord, with the fingering derived from the Form 6 major scale pattern:

The following examples are based on the *Cm7* chord. Notice that the 9th, *D*, is added (alternate fingerings are in parenthesis):

This is based on moving the dominant 7th—the V chord—up the fretboard:

These last patterns are based on the *F7* chord with the added 9th (G) and 13th (D) tones:

This completes the six different fingerings possible for the major scale, as well as the II-V-I chord arpeggios derived from each of those major scale patterns. You have no doubt found that some fingerings feel better than others, and you probably favor certain patterns. At least you have some choices! Remember, the more fingerings you have under your control, the less you will have to jump all over the fingerboard. Next month we'll look at how to use combinations of different fingerings. Till then, "straight ahead."

Arnie Berle's
FRETBOARD BASICS

Reviewing The Major Scales

IN THE SEPTEMBER ISSUE WE COMPLETED THE last of a series of columns illustrating six different possible fingerings for the major scale. Knowing many potential patterns for a particular scale allows you to play anywhere on the fingerboard without having to move your hand a great distance. In other words, by now you should be able to play in any key without moving your hand very far.

Below is a summation of all the scale fingerings we've covered. We'll start with the key of C played with the 4th finger on the 8th fret of the low E string. After that, we will go through all of the major scales.

We'll continue with the rest of the major scales in next month's column. Until then, "straight ahead!"

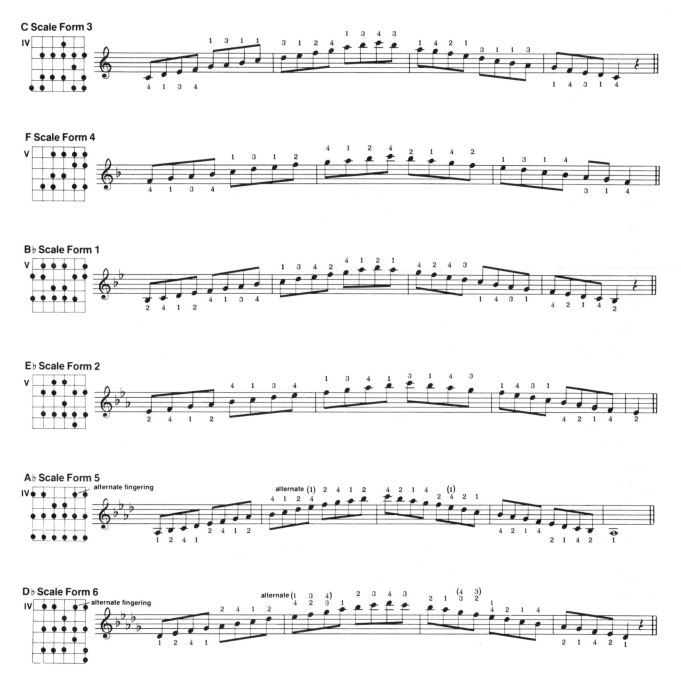

51

Arnie Berle's
FRETBOARD BASICS

December 1982

Playing With Minimum Hand Movement

THIS MONTH WE'LL SHOW HOW IT'S POSSIBLE TO play in all the major keys with a *minimum* of hand movement. In last month's column we played in the keys of *C, F, B♭, E♭, A♭,* and *D♭.* Now we want to continue with the key of *G♭* (or *F♯*). The question is, shall we move to *G♭* starting on the 2nd fret of the sixth string and use the Form 5 fingering, or should we move up to the 9th fret on the fifth string and play in Form 4? Let's try the 2nd fret on the sixth string, as shown in the first scale below.

For the key of *B* we have another choice. Shall we play at the fifth string's 2nd fret and use the Form 6 pattern, or should we move to the 7th fret of the sixth string and try the Form 3 fingering starting with the little finger? Starting on the sixth string results in the least amount of left-hand movement. (It

should be apparent that any given scale may be fingered in several locations on the fretboard.) Be sure to analyze the various fingerboard possibilities for all of the subsequent scales.

This concludes our summation of all the major scale patterns. No doubt you will find some fingerings feel better and "lay" easier than others, but with constant use you should eventually feel comfortable with all six patterns. For years, many fine musicians have concentrated on just a few fingerings, such as the Form 1 and Form 3. Of the six I have presented in this series, you may also decide to concentrate on just a few. Don't be afraid to make adjustments in any fingering to make it easier for yourself. Until next month, "straight ahead."

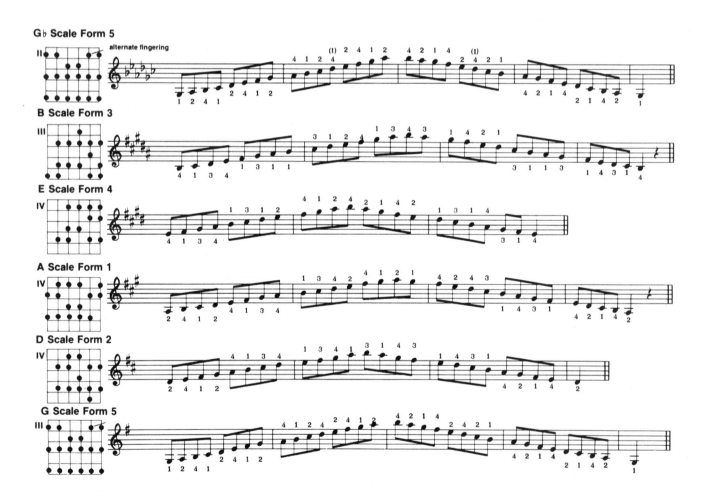

Learning How To Improvise

IT IS AMAZING HOW FAST TIME FLIES WHEN YOU'RE having a ball, and I must say that it is a ball to do these columns and know that so many people are getting something out of them. The mail that comes to my home and the phone calls I get from all over the country make it all worthwhile. I hope everybody had a great holiday, and I wish you all the best for the new year.

Ever since I started writing for *Guitar Player* years ago, I've devoted the January column to answering some of the reader mail I get. Rather than responding to each question separately, I try to address the most often-asked questions. The most common question of them all is: "How do I improvise? I know all my scales, modes, and arpeggios, but I don't know what to do with them. Can you please help me?"

Boy, if I could devise a pill that someone could swallow and learn to play jazz, I'd be a wealthy man overnight. First of all, scales, modes, and arpeggios are only tools. They are important to practice just as a means of developing technique and the ability to get around the fingerboard. They also help you learn where the different tonalities are. As a matter of fact, for the past year I've devoted a lot of my columns to just this issue. From here on in, I will be spending more time trying to help you learn how to develop a jazz solo.

Probably the best thing you can do is what every jazz artist has done: Listen to records. Lennie Tristano, the blind pianist who was a well known and highly respected jazz teacher in '40s and early '50s, would have his students try to sing along with a recording of some great jazz soloist. He would have them try to come as close to the original solo as possible as far as phrasing, inflections, and grace notes. After singing along with the record, the student would have to sing the same solo without the record. Then he would have to work the solo out on his instrument. This regimen would go on for many, many tunes over a long period of time. Hopefully, the student would eventually get to feel as the jazz artist felt when he played the solo, and by osmosis something would rub off on the student. Along with this, of course, the student would have to practice his scales, modes, and arpeggios. It's safe to say that since the beginning of jazz, artists have learned by imitating someone else.

Very soon I will have a new book coming out [to be published by Mel Bay Books, Pacific, MO 63069] called *How To Develop A Jazz Solo*. This book is designed to take the student through a step-by-step regimen for composing solos. Another important project that a jazz student could do is simply to learn by ear as many tunes as possible. Playing the same tunes in many different keys is very good for developing the ear. Trying to write down tunes that you hear is also an excellent ear-training device. Learn to play a number of different patterns that may be applied over the more commonly used progressions, such as the II-V-I. You can also purchase some books containing transcribed solos by the great jazz artists. Music Sales Corp. [33 West 60th St., New York, NY 10023] has a number of very fine books with transcriptions of solos by Charlie Parker, Miles Davis, Benny Goodman, and other jazz greats. Each book includes an analysis of what the soloist was trying to do. When you practice these, be sure to study the notes in relation to the chord symbols.

There are also a number of fine rhythm records that allow students to play to prerecorded jazz accompaniments. These give you a chance to hear what the chord progressions of different tunes sound like. It's important that the jazz player be able to recognize the more common progressions found in jazz tunes. Guitarists have an advantage over horn players because they can play a tune's chords while singing a jazz solo. Listen to the quality of each chord and try to match your singing to that quality. Later try to locate on the fingerboard the notes that you were singing.

Studying theory will give you a good understanding of the modern chords that you might come across. This way, if your ear fails you, you can rely on your knowledge to get you through a solo. It is very important to understand that becoming a competent jazz player requires lots of patience and time; it simply doesn't happen fast. You must constantly work on improving your technique so that you can execute your ideas smoothly without having to grope for notes. Another way to save time and quicken your progress is to organize your practice time so that you get the best results. Allow definite portions of time for scale work, arpeggios, singing along with recorded solos, and memorizing patterns based on common chord progressions.

I hope that I have given you some ideas on how to train yourself to be a jazz player. My next series of columns will be devoted to the same subject. Until next month, "straight ahead."

Arnie Berle's
FRETBOARD BASICS

February 1983

Variations On The II-V-I Progression

LAST MONTH WE COMPLETED A RATHER LENGTHY series of columns showing six different ways of fingering major scales and the very important minor 7th (II chord), dominant 7th (V chord), and the major 7th (I chord). We also extended each of these chords up to 9ths and 13ths. Now is a good time to solidify what we've learned by playing the II, V, and I chords as progressions rather than as isolated arpeggios. As we'll see, these may be played with the various fingerings examined in previous columns. And if you don't know all of the fingerings for arpeggios, this will be a good review. Let's start with the II-V-I chords in the key of *C* and see how many ways we can finger the progression practically.

This Form 1 pattern lays well on the fingerboard:

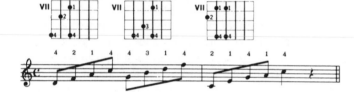

Form 2 is okay, but watch the shift in fingering the *B* string, or use the alternate fingering in parentheses:

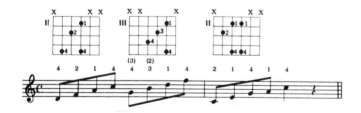

The Form 3 pattern lays very well:

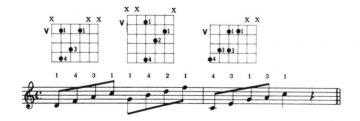

Form 4 requires a cutaway guitar, since it's played high up the neck. It would be more practical in a key played lower on the neck:

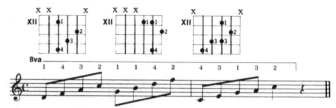

Form 5 is okay, but watch the stretches:

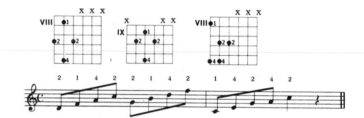

Form 6 also lays well, but again, take care with the stretches:

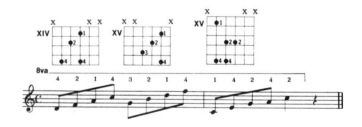

Now that you know how to finger the II-V-I progression six different ways, try to play the same progression in other keys, using as many different patterns as you can. Until next time, "straight ahead."

Arnie Berle's
FRETBOARD BASICS

How Can I Improvise?

THE NEXT FEW COLUMNS WILL ANSWER MANY letters I've received from readers who write, "I know all my scales and arpeggios, but I don't know how to improvise. Can you help me?" At the outset, I'd like to say that all any teacher can do is provide the techniques and some of the devices that are used by the great jazz players. Beyond that, no teacher can make someone creative if they are not naturally that way.

Obviously, there are a number of approaches to teaching improvisation. One disadvantage I face when teaching through a column is that I don't have the luxury of being in a one-on-one situation with you, such as in a private lesson, where a teacher can evaluate where you stand and know which approach is best suited for your particular needs. Another risk I run is that if I make the material too easy, I'm going to bore a lot of readers. If I make it too advanced, I'm going to turn off a lot of readers. So I think we'll start with an approach to improvisation that will be easy enough for the beginner, while still providing more advanced players with a good review of techniques.

Before we begin, it is important that you have down most of the six available fingerings for all the major scales, as well as the major 7th, minor 7th, and dominant 7th chord arpeggios. These were all covered in my last series of columns.

The simplest approach to improvisation is to begin by using only the notes of the chords. For our examples, we will use the very common I-VI-II-V chord progression, although this approach works for any progression, including blues. Play through the chords using half notes. Try to connect the chords as smoothly as possible. Notice that in the following examples, each four-measure example starts on a different note within the I chord. Play each example using as many different fingerings as you can:

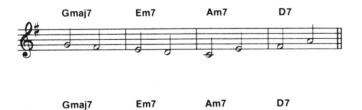

This next exercise is based on quarter notes played through the chords. This is especially good, since you have to think a little faster to play quarter notes:

After you are comfortable playing the examples I have given you, apply the same formula to any progression of your choice. Start first with half notes, and when you can do those well, move on to quarter notes. The main idea is to be able to move from chord to chord in a smooth, connected manner without stopping. If you can create little melodies as you play through the chords, it will even be better. We will continue this subject next month. Till then, "straight ahead."

55

Arnie Berle's
FRETBOARD BASICS

Improvisation: Don't Limit Yourself

LAST MONTH WE BEGAN A SERIES OF COLUMNS ON how to develop improvisational techniques. For now, we will concentrate on just playing through the chords using *only* chord tones—that is, the notes within the chord. Our example is the I-VI-II-V progression in the key of *G: Gmaj7, Em7, Am7, D7*. In April we started with half notes in order to give ourselves time to think, and then we graduated to quarter notes. Now we will go through the chords using eighth notes:

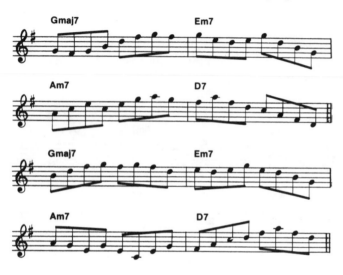

Remember, you can apply this improvisational approach to the chords or progressions of any tune. The next example is based on triplets:

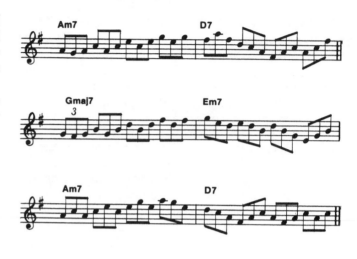

This uses sixteenth-notes:

For your own good, try to play each of the examples using as many fingerings as you can. Don't limit yourself to just playing in *G* or any other key in only one area of the fingerboard. As we've seen in past columns, there are six different ways to play in any key. Next month we'll go on with our study of improvisation. Until then, "straight ahead."

Arnie Berle's
FRETBOARD BASICS

Improving Your Improvisation

IN THIS SERIES OF COLUMNS WE WILL TRY TO ANSWER some questions about improvising. First, it is important to understand just what is meant by "improvising." The most commonly used definition describes it as the spontaneous creation of melodies based on a given series of chords. Simply put, this means that at the spur of the moment you should be able to make up melodies that are related to the notes suggested by the given chord progression. Now, it's true that in recent years the word improvisation has taken on new meanings, particularly as a result of saxophonist Ornette Coleman and others in the free jazz movement who do not use any restrictions as to chords or even bar lines. It's music that's based, as Coleman says, "on the emotions" of the piece, not the background. Since I do not want to get into any discussion of the merits or demerits of this style of improvisation, we will stick with the more conventional meaning of improvisation in these columns.

In our first column of this series (April '83), we showed how to connect a melody through a I-VI-II-V progression. We started out using only half notes, and then went on to quarter notes. In the May column we played through the same progression using eighth-notes, then finally triplets and sixteenth-notes. This month we will combine the various note values into one improvisation. Remember that these are not intended to be examples of great jazz. Our immediate goal is to just be able to move through a given set of chords. For now, we will further restrict ourselves by using *only* chord tones.

After playing through these examples, you should be able to make up your own improvisations based on the same or any other set of chords, such as progressions for blues or standards. But first follow the regimen given in these columns and don't be in a hurry or let yourself become discouraged. Right now these will sound like exercises, but as you add more notes, your creative possibilities will come through. The first three examples are in the key of *G*, which can be played in a number of different positions. I would suggest you start off with the Form 1 scale fingering shown here:

Form 1 G Scale

Use the above fingering to locate all of the notes in the following examples. Also try playing them in other positions.

The next two examples are in the key of *C*. Here you should use the Form 2 fingering. Notice, however, that the *B* in measure 4 must be reached by stretching. You might try playing it with the Form 1 *C* pattern up on the 8th fret, or the Form 3 pattern beginning with the 4th finger at the 8th fret. Here are the fingerings:

Form 2 C Scale   Form 3 C Scale

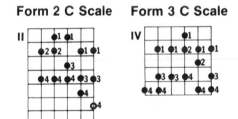

These examples in the key of *C* can use either of the fingerings given above:

Remember that you must make up your own examples of improvisation using combinations of rhythms as shown above. Use only chord tones and any series of chords you want. Next month we'll take this one step further. Until then, "straight ahead."

Arnie Berle's
FRETBOARD BASICS

Rhythmic Phrasing

LAST MONTH I COMBINED HALF NOTES, EIGHTH-notes, sixteenth notes, and triplets in several exercises. This month let's move ahead to the next step in developing a jazz solo: rhythmic phrasing.

If you examine a great jazz player's solos you will find he knows exactly when to put breathing spaces—rests—in an improvisation. Rests give a solo *shape*. While many inexperienced guitarists try to throw in everything they know because they want to impress the listener, the experienced musician is more concerned with making a musical statement. The great tenor sax man Lester Young used to say that his solos told a story. Using rests emphasizes your phrases and gives the listener time to digest what you are saying musically. Carefully study the following series of two-measure rhythm patterns, which include rests both on and off the beat. While there are many different rhythm patterns, the ones shown here are frequently found in jazz solos:

Here are some one-measure patterns that work well at slower tempos and use sixteenth-notes:

The preceding exercises are shown with only one note so that you can concentrate on the rhythms only. Be sure to memorize them as soon as possible. Next month we'll apply these patterns to the I VI II V progression. Until then, "straight ahead."

58

Arnie Berle's
FRETBOARD BASICS

September 1983

Developing Jazz Phrases

LAST MONTH I PRESENTED A SERIES OF RHYTHM patterns so you could see how space—rests—can be used in improvising. Now let's apply those rhythms to a I VI II V progression in the key of *G*.

Play the following examples using different fingerings and areas of the fingerboard:

The next examples should be played slow and relaxed. Be sure not to rush the sixteenth-notes. Notice that a different one-measure rhythm pattern from last month's lesson is used for each chord in the progression:

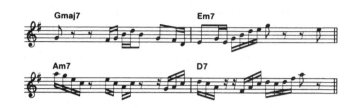

This last fragment employs two chords per measure. Start slowly in order to get used to changing chords in the middle of a phrase:

At this point start inventing your own improvisations based on the preceding rhythm patterns (keep things simple at first by using chord tones only). Also, take rhythm patterns from solos by your favorite players and apply your own notes. Next month we'll begin to add more notes to our phrases. Until then, "straight ahead."

59

Arnie Berle's
FRETBOARD BASICS

October 1983

The Scalar Approach

THIS SERIES OF COLUMNS ON jazz improvisation has focused on improvising with chord tones only. Obviously, using only chord tones places a limit on the number of musical ideas possible. But remember that what we are doing is necessary in learning to develop melodic lines.

Inventor Thomas Edison said, "Genius is 99% perspiration and 1% inspiration." Any of you who have read interviews with jazz guitarists such as Tal Farlow or Barney Kessel know that they spent years practicing. Most listeners don't stop to consider the vast amount of time behind a seemingly effortless solo. All the talent in the world doesn't mean a thing if you don't develop the mechanical skills that will enable your ideas to emerge. Saxophonist John Coltrane was a fanatic about practicing scales and even went over them between sets at clubs. It often annoys me to learn that some "star" who never practiced makes a lot of money.

At this point you should be using my examples of improvisations as a practice guide. Take your favorite standards and employ the exercises I've outlined in the past few columns. Practice arpeggiating through all the harmonies, using different rhythmic values such as half notes, quarter notes, eighth-notes, triplets, and sixteenths. Then use them in various combinations and apply some of the rhythms using rests. In addition, you should be copying rhythmic patterns off of records.

The next step in learning to improvise is to follow the same system that we used with chord tones. We know that all chords come from scales, so we're going to develop some lines to fit the I VI II V progression. The major scale is used for the I chord. (If you have been doing your homework and have been following my

previous columns, you are able to play major scales in several fingerboard locations. The scale that fits the VI chord (m7) is called the aeolian mode, and starts on the sixth note of a major scale (see Ex. 1). Ex. 2 shows the dorian mode, which fits the II (m7) chord and starts on the second note of the major scale. The scale for the V chord is the mixolydian mode (Ex. 3), which starts on the fifth note.

At this point you would be right in asking why we don't just use the major scale to play through the complete I VI II V progression. The answer is that you could, but music has to have a sense of forward motion—a sense of resolving to the I chord. For example, if you're improvising on a G7 chord and just play the C scale, what happens when you reach the tonic chord? There is no sense of tension and resolution—a sense of having gone anywhere. It's like a fighter who gives away his punches. You want

to play a scale on the G7 that sounds like it wants to move to the C.

You can say that the G mixolydian mode is the C scale starting from G. But when we play a particular scale, we tend to emphasize the 1st, 3rd, 5th, and 7th notes of that scale—the harmony. If we use the G mixolydian mode we will tend to place greater emphasis on the notes G, B, D, and F. Those tones have a tendency to lead to the C chord (tonic). If we play the C scale for the G7, then we might tend to emphasize the notes C, E, G, and B. Many jazz players use scales other than the mixolydian mode for dominant chords, because they want to create even more tension.

Next month we'll take a look at the scales for the I VI II V progression. For an in-depth study of this subject, see my new book called *How To Create And Develop A Jazz Solo,* published by Mel Bay. Until then, "straight ahead."

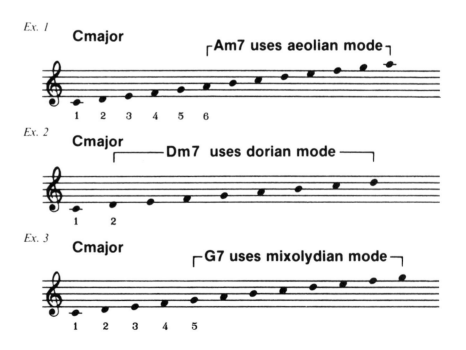

Ex. 1 Cmajor — Am7 uses aeolian mode

Ex. 2 Cmajor — Dm7 uses dorian mode

Ex. 3 Cmajor — G7 uses mixolydian mode

60

Arnie Berle's
FRETBOARD BASICS

Scalar Improvising

LAST MONTH WE STARTED PUTTING CHORDS BACK INTO scales (previous columns dealt with improvising using arpeggios, as opposed to scales). This month let's continue to explore the scalar approach to improvising.

Remember that learning scales and how to use them takes disciplined study. And when a jazz player improvises, he doesn't make a conscious decision to play either all chord tones or all scale tones. The talented veteran jazz guitarist Gene Bertoncini (profiled in the October '77 issue of *Guitar Player)* says that eventually the intellectualization process will become intuitive.

First, let's review the material we covered last month. Here are the scales for the I VI II V chords in the key of *C*:

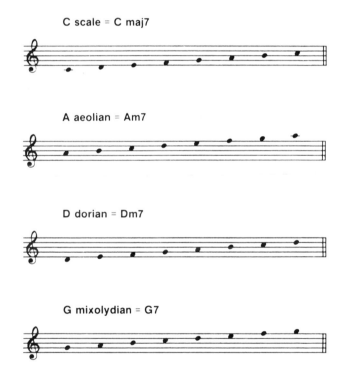

Now let's take a look at some two- and four-bar examples of an improvised line (it's important to get used to playing both). Note that each phrase uses eighth-notes exclusively:

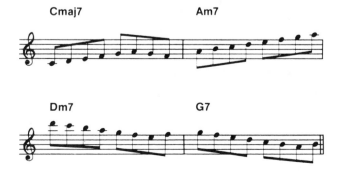

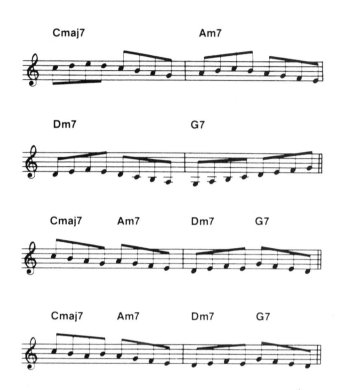

Working on triplets can help you to develop longer lines. Start with these examples and then invent some of your own:

Some of the preceding improvisations may sound a bit bland since we are limiting ourselves only to scale tones. But be patient and work on your technique and getting familiar with the material at hand. Soon we'll be adding neighboring tones, scale substitutes, and various rhythms—musical spice. Until next time, "straight ahead."

Arnie Berle's
FRETBOARD BASICS

Sixteenth-Note Improvisation

THIS LAST YEAR HAS REALLY PASSED QUICKLY: I hope you're working hard and getting the full benefit from my latest columns on improvisation. From the mail I've received, it seems that many of you are. To those of you who are already good improvisers, I suggest that it might not be a bad idea to try to follow the course I've laid out in this latest series. You might get some new ideas and learn a different approach to creating improvised lines.

Over the last couple of months we've been studying short examples of improvised lines featuring scale tones. Remember that you eventually should use the principles outlined here for complete tunes. In other words, try expanding our two- and four-bar ideas to a 12-bar blues or to the standard 32-bar form.

In our last lesson we improvised on the I VI II V progression in the key of *C* using only scale tones. For the sake of simplicity, the exercises used either eighth-notes or eighth note triplets. Now let's take a look at some examples using sixteenth-notes. A good general rule is to have a chord tone on the strong beats (first and third) of the measure. This enables a scale-oriented line to keep its tonal identity. Notice the chordal tones used in Ex. 1.

Ex. 2 uses two chords in each measure. Again, notice how the root of each chord comes in on the first and third beats (remember this could be any chord tone).

The two- and four-bar examples of scalar improvisation in Ex. 3 combine eighth-notes, triplets, and sixteenth-notes.

Next month I'll try to answer some reader questions. Until then, "straight ahead."

62

Creative Scale Construction

ONCE AGAIN, IT'S THE START OF A NEW YEAR. THIS month I'd like to take a break from my current series on improvisation to express my appreciation of the *Guitar Player* staff, who edits my column and sees that it's put together right. And, of course, there would be no magazine without the readers. I wish them all the best and would especially like to thank the ones who take the time to send in their helpful questions and comments.

Over the years I've had the honor to meet and learn from many great guitarists, such as Herb Ellis, Barney Kessel, Jimmy Raney, Tal Farlow, and Kenny Burrell. It's very instructive for me to probe their minds and gain insight into the mysteries of the creative process. These men are all very knowledgeable about music and have obviously done their homework. However, a lot of guitarists—especially rock players—play strictly by ear and intuition and can't talk much about the theoretical side of music (although David Spinoza and Elliot Randall— two top studio rock players—know all about the technical side of music). Remember, the more you know about something, the better off you'll be.

My current series on improvisation is bringing in many letters with questions on scales and their place in improvisation. Young guitarists are very much interested in learning scales, and the schools that teach jazz are turning out lots of guitarists who play them really well. But although they tear up and down their instruments with great speed, as Barney Kessel once said, "I don't hear any jazz."

There is so much more to playing creative jazz than just knowing a lot of scales. Some time ago the fine jazz guitarist Howie Collins (who I interviewed in the October 1979 issue of *Guitar Player)* asked if he could come by my studio and discuss some of the different scales that his students were asking him about—the lydian ♭7, the super locrian, the lydian augmented, etc. I told him that he was playing those scales (or the notes in all of those scales) already except that he wasn't thinking in those terms. He was naturally hearing those sounds in his head and playing them. Placing interesting, dissonant, tension producing notes in scale patterns is just a device—a practical tool—for those who can't hear the notes naturally.

Please understand that I'm not putting down learning these scales. If you follow my present series on improvisation, you'll see that I will cover them. As a matter of fact, I have written books on those scales, and I believe they have a very definite purpose.

However, they're given too much emphasis. Remember, it's the feeling that counts. A hundred notes in a bar played without any feeling of good rhythmic placement is nowhere near as good as four well-placed notes.

Since we're getting near the end of this column, let me leave you with something to try on your guitar and think about. If you've been following my columns regularly, you should know the fingerings for a number of different 7th chords. First play a *C7* arpeggio (*C, E, G, B♭*). Then play a *D7* arpeggio (*D, F♯, A, C*). Now intermingle the two arpeggios and listen to the result:

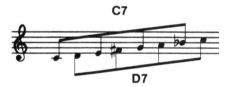

Now try the same thing with the *C7* and *Dmaj7* arpeggios:

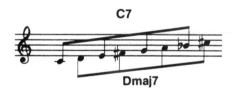

The next example combines the *C7* and *D7♭5*. First play them as arpeggios and then put them together into one scale:

Do you see how it's possible to make up your own scales? These are legitimate scales, but if I gave you their names you would only be confused. Next month we'll answer some letters from readers. Until then, "straight ahead."

Arnie Berle's
FRETBOARD BASICS

February 1984

Combining Arpeggios To Create Scales

LAST MONTH I DIGRESSED FROM MY RECENT SERIES OF columns on improvising to make a few personal comments on scales and playing in general. This month I'd like to address an aspect of improvising with scales that readers ask me about in their many letters. Next month we'll return to the subject of soloing.

I concluded the last lesson by showing how you can combine two different chords to create a scale. The following sequence features the notes of the *C7* and *D7* arpeggios:

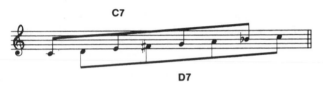

The above series of tones is often referred to as either the lydian ♭7 scale or the lydian dominant scale. But more important than the name is to know how a tonal series is formed and used. It's formed by combining two dominant 7th chords whose roots are a whole-step apart. It can be used for either a *C7, a C9♯11,* or a *C13♯11.* (The *F♯* note in the scale is the ♯11, the *A* is the 13th, and the *D* is the 9th.)

If you add a *Dmaj7 arpeggio* to the notes of a *C7* chord, you produce the following sequence, which is often called the altered dominant scale:

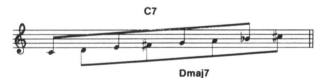

This series fits a *C7,* a *C7♭9♯11,* and a *C13♭9♯11.* (The *C♯* is the flatted ninth.)

An interesting scale results when you combine the *C7add6* and the *E♭m7* arpeggios:

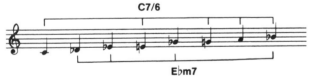

This creates another form of the altered dominant scale. A closer look will also tell you that it's the *half-step/whole-step* diminished pattern. Both the ♭9 and the ♯9 are contained in the scale. Consequently, it could be used with any chord that has those notes. If superimposed over a plain dominant 7th chord, it will provide the kind of tension frequently heard in jazz.

At this point you should try creating your own scales by combining different chords. Remember that the names of the scales aren't as important as knowing how to produce the sounds you want. I'm sure that alto sax genius Charlie Parker didn't know the names of all these different scales, but he certainly did know how to produce and to use them. I strongly urge you to study the solos of Parker, as well as those of other bebop masters, including pianist Bud Powell and trumpeter Dizzy Gillespie. After all, jazz is a musical language and its vocabulary must be thoroughly studied. Styles such as swing, bop, and modal jazz all have their own cliches. And once you get their sounds in your head and can analyze them, you'll eventually find yourself speaking the language.

Before I close off the subject of scales for this month, I want to talk a bit about one scale that doesn't have an exotic name, but is one of the most important: the chromatic scale. It consists of all half-steps and can start on any note. The chromatic scale has the advantage of being used with *any* chord type and with any combination of altered tones. But be careful of its overuse. Too much chromaticism tends to detract from the jazz style. Also, there will always be some scale tone that will clash with the basic chord. This problem can be solved by moving either up or down a half-step to the nearest chord tone.

Here are some examples of the use of chromatic runs applied to some common progressions. Notice how Parker was not afraid to play basic chord tones, as in the first of the following two measures:

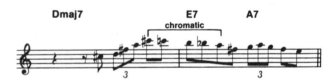

In the next phrase, note how Parker used the ♭9 even though the basic chord is A7:

Here he uses the ♭9 with a chromatic series in the first bar, while the second measure is made up of chord tones only:

This last example features a chromatic run that ascends and then descends:

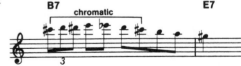

If you have any questions, feel free to write to me in care of *Guitar Player,* 20085 Stevens Creek, Cupertino, CA 95014. Until next month, "straight ahead."

64

Arnie Berle's
FRETBOARD BASICS

Jazz Phrasing

AFTER TAKING A BREAK IN MY JANUARY AND FEBRU-ary columns from my series on improvising, let's return to learning how to develop a jazz solo. In December I gave you some examples of improvisations based on the I VI II V progression, which used only scale tones, and combined eighth-notes, triplets, and sixteenth-notes. This month we'll add some more complex figures to our rhythmic vocabulary.

The following one-measure rhythm patterns use rests on different beats. Concentrate on learning each figure by playing them exactly as written—with the *C* note only:

The next step is to apply the preceding patterns to the I VI II V progression and create a line made up of only scale tones. Eventually when you do your improvisations you should use either a blues progression or the chords to a jazz standard. Note that the following two examples are in the keys of *C* and *G*, respectively:

While the previous phrases used one chord per measure, these employ two:

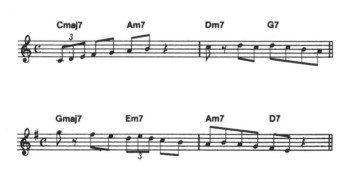

The following six patterns have a double-time feel and work best when the tempo is slower and you want to fill up the measure with a lot of notes:

The next examples make use of the preceding rhythmic figures (note the phrases with two chords per measure):

One general rule is to try to have a chord tone played on the first and third beats of each measure. But keep in mind that this is not always possible since we're restricted to playing scale tones only. Next month we'll combine chord and scale tones and learn how to make our solos more interesting by introducing chromatic tones, substitute scales, and blues phrases. Until then, remember—straight ahead.

Arnie Berle's
FRETBOARD BASICS

Developing Complex Phrasing

FOR THE PAST SEVERAL MONTHS I'VE KEPT THINGS simple by restricting the material to chord and scale tones. (Keep in mind that jazz players don't really limit themselves when improvising. They use whatever they hear in their heads, and try to play what they feel.) Also, the last several columns have used fairly straightforward rhythmic patterns. If you've been listening to jazz artists (on all instruments), then your ear has absorbed many, many additional phrases. Rock players, who tend to stick with basic rhythms, will especially benefit from these new patterns.

If you've been taking licks off records or learning from some of the many good books of transcriptions available, you'll see (as well as hear) that although jazz is a complex form, it still uses certain patterns. The following examples combine chord and scale tones. Listen for familiar sequences:

These lines employ two chords per measure (be sure to play the changes in order to better hear how the notes relate to the harmonies):

If you're thinking the preceding examples sound a little colorless, you're right. They sound the way a bowl of plain yogurt tastes. But if you start adding fruit, it'll really jazz things up. The blues scale (root ♭3 4 ♭5 5 ♭7) is one element that can really lend a new

dimension to soloing. Historically, certain tones considered to be out of pitch by European classical standards came to be called "blue" notes, and were a carryover from African vocal traditions. Guitarists, of course, could produce these notes by bending the strings, while reed and brass players got blues sounds by certain lipping techniques. Eventually the blues scale became recognized as an integral part of American music, and one of the first devices used to create a jazzier sound.

Remember that the blues scale is not necessarily used only with a blues progression (note that one scale will fit every chord in a I IV V 12-bar sequence). Jazz players often use blue notes to lend a blues feeling to *any* sequence of chords.

You can find fingerings for the blues scale by using familiar major scale patterns as a starting point and making adjustments as necessary. The following example shows the blues scale written in the keys of *C* and *G*. Try finding them in as many positions as possible:

This fingering is the one most favored by rock and blues players. It's easy to execute and can be used in different keys just by moving it up or down the fingerboard:

G Blues Scale

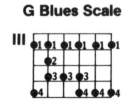

If blues scales are new to you, make learning them a priority. Once you have a fingering down, try inventing some phrases. *[Ed. Note: For more on the blues scale, see Rik Emmett's Back To Basics column in the March '83 issue.]* If properly used, this scale can be a very effective way of adding interest to a jazz solo. Next month we'll continue our exploration of the blues scale. Until then, "straight ahead."

Arnie Berle's
FRETBOARD BASICS

Blues Spice

FOR IMPROVISATION, THE BLUES SCALE WORKS BEST when it's used with a basic I IV V blues progression. But it may also be played over a IIm7 V7 sequence. For this type of application, use the blues scale with the same tonic as the chord. In other words, use the D blues scale for the Dm7 chord, and the G blues scale for the G7 chord. (See last month's column for the blues scale's structure.)

The following examples use the familiar I VI II V progression. These phrases are based on the ones shown last month, only I've added some blue notes to make them sound more spicy:

Remember that the blue notes are the ♭3, ♭5, and ♭7 of the major scale. If you want to add blue notes to a IIm7 chord, all you have to think about is flatting the 5th, because the 7th and the 3rd are naturally lowered. For instance, when playing against a Dm7 chord, include the A♭ (for the G7, add the B♭ and the D♭). In the preceding exercises, notice how the blue notes are mixed in with the normal notes of the scale.

Last month I presented the following common fingering for the blues scale:

F blues scale

Another related scale is shown in the next example. Notice the similarity to the preceding pattern. This fingering can be called by either of two names: F minor pentatonic or A♭ major pentatonic:

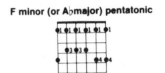
F minor (or A♭major) pentatonic

Now let's compare the F blues scale, the F minor pentatonic scale, and the A♭ major pentatonic scale:

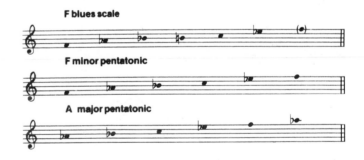

The difference between the blues scale and the minor pentatonic scale is that the blues scale contains the ♭5. Also notice that the minor pentatonic and the major pentatonic contain exactly the same notes but start on different roots. When using the blues scale (or the minor pentatonic) with a basic I IV V progression, be sure to use the scale with the same name as the key the tune is in. For example, in the key of F, use either the F blues scale or the F minor pentatonic. A word of caution: When you use blue notes with progressions other than the blues, be careful not to throw in tones out of the clear blue sky just to show off. Always use good taste, and make whatever you play fit into a solo logically. Next month we'll take a look at more ways to make a solo sound interesting. Until then, "straight ahead."

Arnie Berle's
FRETBOARD BASICS

Know Your Neighbors

ONE OF THE BEST WAYS TO ADD VARIETY TO A solo is to utilize neighboring notes, found above and below each chord tone. The lower neighbor is the note one half-step below the chord tone, and the upper neighbor is the next scale tone above. The following examples of lower and upper neighbors are based on the I VI II V progression. Carefully analyze each phrase, and practice playing neighboring tones on all major 7th, minor 7th, and dominant 7th harmonies.

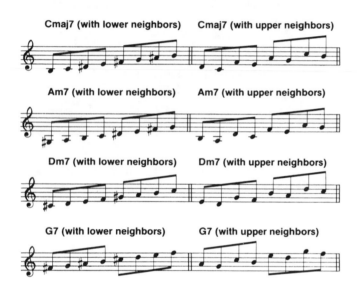

The next example shows lower and upper neighboring tones in various combinations for the *Cmaj7* chord.

In most scales, any note can be embellished with neighbors. The following patterns are based on the *C* major scale:

Once you have a few sequences with neighboring notes under your fingers, apply them to a progression. To get you started, here are a few lines for the I VI II V progression:

Next month we'll explore some more ways to add color to an improvisation. Until then, "straight ahead."

Arnie Berle's
FRETBOARD BASICS

July 1984

Diminished Chord Concepts

MY LATEST SERIES OF COLUMNS CONCERNS VARIOUS ways to make an improvised line more interesting. In the April and May issues, I discussed the blues scale, while the June installment looked at neighboring tones—notes above and below each degree of a chord or scale. This month is devoted to another common improvisational device: the diminished chord. Because the diminished chord can be used in so many different soloing situations, it is one of the most interesting sources of melodic material. *[Ed. Note: For an in-depth study of chord structures, see Chord Construction Primer in the June 1981 issue; for a look at developing diminished-based dominant 7th licks, see Tal Farlow's Private Lesson on page 68.]*

The following example shows a diminished arpeggio and block chord. (While B♭♭ is the technically correct way of notating the fourth note of the *C* diminished arpeggio, *A* is commonly used, because it doesn't require sharps or flats.) Since the diminished chord is constructed solely of minor-third intervals, each note can be considered to be the root. The *Cdim7* chord can also be called *E♭dim7, G♭dim7 (or F♯dim7), or Adim7.*

Now let's take a look at some diminished chord fingerings. Again, it's very important to understand that each chord has four names. The following fingering can be called *F♯dim7, E♭dim7, Adim7,* or *Cdim7.* Practice moving it up the fretboard, taking care to analyze the resulting chords.

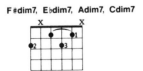

Here are two more common fingerings for the diminished 7th chord:

Play each of the preceding chord forms up the fingerboard, and recite their four names at each fret.

Turning our attention from block chords to arpeggios, learn the following fingering and play it up the fingerboard:

The preceding pattern can be broken into smaller units:

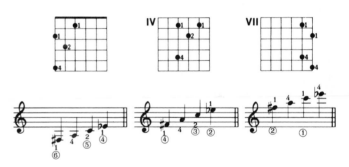

This useful fingering moves up the fretboard quickly and requires only two left-hand fingers:

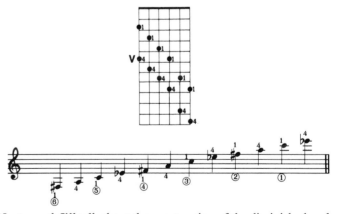

Next month I'll talk about the construction of the diminished scale and how it can be applied to soloing. Until next time, "straight ahead."

Arnie Berle's
FRETBOARD BASICS

Diminished Scale Improv

NOW THAT YOU HAVE A GRASP OF DIMINISHED CHORDS and arpeggios (last month's topic), let's turn our attention to the diminished scale, which is constructed like so: W (whole-step) H (half-step) W H W H W H. *[Ed. Note: For more on the diminished scale, see Scale Systems in the July 1984 issue of* Guitar Player.*]* Observe that when you build the scale in this manner, you are simply adding a note that's one whole-step above each chordal tone. In the following example, each arpeggio note is circled:

Due to its symmetrical, whole-/half-step structure, each diminished scale has *four* possible names. Here are two more diminished patterns, which have a total of eight different roots:

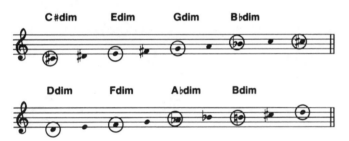

Left-hand fingerings coinciding with last month's arpeggios can readily be developed. The following diagrams show a fingering for the F#dim7 arpeggio and its coinciding scale. The three diminished chord forms presented last month can be found within these patterns.

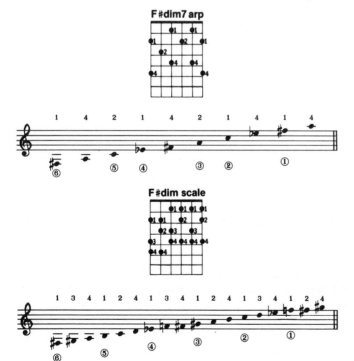

Here are two fingerings that move lengthwise along the fingerboard:

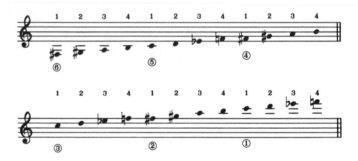

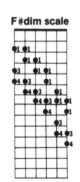

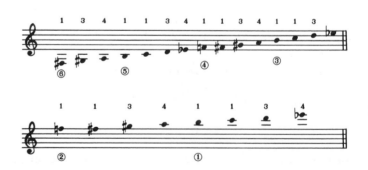

Be sure to approach the preceding material a little at a time learning each fingering thoroughly. Next month, I'll explore various ways the diminished scale is used for soloing. Until then, "straight ahead."

Arnie Berle's
FRETBOARD BASICS

September 1984

Diminished Scale Applications

FOR THE PAST TWO MONTHS, I'VE BEEN DISCUSSING diminished arpeggios and scales, as well as how this important tonal sequence is fingered. Now let's learn how the diminished scale can be applied to improvising.

In jazz, the diminished scale is commonly used to improvise over the diminished chord of the same name. The following example shows the F#dim 7 chord being used in a progression that goes I #Idim7 II V. (The #Idim7 connects the I to the II.)

However, another way in which jazz players use the diminished scale is to superimpose it over dominant 7th chords. While this usage is a bit more complicated than the preceding application, it is an important part of an improvisor's vocabulary that can add a great deal of color to a solo. To improvise over a dominant 7th chord, use the diminished scale whose tonic (root) is a half-step higher than the tonic of the dominant 7th chord. For example, use the C#diminished scale for C7. Here are the notes of the C# diminished scale in relation to C7:

Notice that the diminished scale contains the ♭9, #9, and ♭5 of the dominant 7th chord whose tonic is a half-step lower. These tones are invaluable to adding interesting tension to a solo.

One of the best ways to study how diminished scales work for dominant 7th chords is to play them in a progression. The following examples feature a V I sequence—G7 to C; the A♭ dim7 scale is used for the G7:

The diminished scale can also be used with the II V progression. Here are some examples of the A♭ diminished scale superimposed over a II V I in C major:

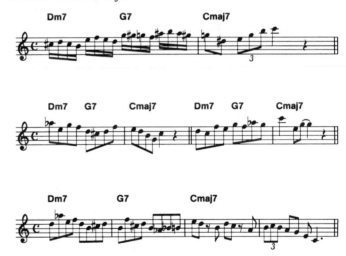

Last month, we learned that each diminished scale has four possible names; therefore, the A♭ diminished scale can also be called the D diminished scale. For a II V progression, use the diminished scale whose name corresponds to that of the II chord (note that the same scale can be continued for the V). For example, in the key of C, use the D diminished scale for Dm 7 to G7 (II V); in the key of F, use G diminished for Gm7 to C7, etc.

Because some of the notes of the diminished scale clash with certain chords, try not to linger on the "outside" tones too long (no more than an eighth-note). Of course, the more you work with diminished scales, the sooner you'll be able to sense what sounds good. Next month, we'll further explore this interesting and important melodic device. Until then, "straight ahead."

Arnie Berle's
FRETBOARD BASICS

October 1984

Diminished Scale Licks

THE DIMINISHED SCALE CAN BE USED IN MANY DIFFER-
ent ways because it has a symmetrical structure, which results in it
having four different roots (see my July through Sept. '84 columns).
For example, a *C* diminished scale is also an *Eb, Gb* and *Ab*
diminished scale. While the diminished scale fits the diminished
chord, it can also be superimposed over dominant 7th harmonies.
This can be achieved by using the scale whose root is one half-step
higher than the dominant chord you want to improvise over. Consequently, one diminished lick can fit four dominant chords, giving
you a great deal of versatility when soloing.

The following lick is based on the *C* diminished scale (also the *Eb,
Gb,* and *Ab* diminished scales). Since it has four different names and
can be used in four different ways, I have shown it resolving to four
different tonic chords. The numbers beneath each lick illustrate the
relationship of the phrase in terms of the dominant chord it's being
superimposed over. To better help you hear how diminished lines
sound, I strongly recommend that you either tape the changes or
have a friend play them. When you use the same lick in several
different ways, some applications sound better than others; however, all fit.

The following phrase is based on the *C#* diminished scale (also *E, G,*
and *Bb*), and can be played over the *C7, Eb7, F#7,* and *A7* chords.

Depending on the dominant harmony you're playing over, it can
resolve to either *F, Ab, B,* or *D* major.

This sequence is based on the *D* diminished scale (also *F, Ab,* or *B*
diminished), and can be played over a *C#7, E7, G7,* or *Bb7* chord.
As in the preceding example, it can resolve to four major tonalities.

Creating your own licks based on the diminished scale is relatively
easy. Many diminished scale fingerings feature repeating patterns.
Note the alternating 1-3-4 1-2-4 fingerings in the following diagram:

This lick came about by experimenting with the preceding fingering
on the top two strings. I added the third string to continue the
sequence:

Using the same fingerings on the same string can produce some
interesting sequences. This one ascends in minor third intervals:

Here's an eight-note repeating pattern on the third string:

Remember: The key to coming up with new licks and ways to use
them is patience; experimenting with musical ideas never stops.
Until next month, "straight ahead."

Arnie Berle's
FRETBOARD BASICS

Superimposing The Jazz Minor Scale

TO IMPROVISE EFFECTIVELY, merely knowing scales is not enough: You must be able to use them. Over the last four months, I've covered the diminished scale and how its use with dominant chords produces one of the most common jazz sounds. This month, let's discuss the jazz minor scale, which should be included in every modern guitarist's musical vocabulary.

As you already know, in relation to *G7,* the *A♭* diminished scale has three highly colorful, tension-producing tones: ♭9, ♯9, and ♭5 (see my July through October '84 columns). For years, jazz musicians have used the diminished scale in this manner to create hip, dissonant melodies. Another equally useful way to generate altered dominant sounds is to superimpose the jazz minor scale (the same as the ascending melodic minor; see the Scale Systems feature in the July 1984 issue). When the *A♭* jazz minor scale is played over *G7, four* altered notes in addition to the lowered 7th are produced: ♭9, ♯9, ♭5, and ♯5. *[Ed. Note: Playing the A♭ ascending melodic minor scale from G to G produces the superlocrian mode. For more information on this subject, see Larry Coryell's column on page 130.]*

In case your knowledge of minor scales is a bit sketchy, let's briefly review the three most common ones. Perhaps the most frequently used minor scale is the natural minor, which has a lowered 3rd, 6th, and 7th. In Ex. l, notice that *A* natural minor is related to the key of C major, and starts on its sixth note, *A*. The natural minor is also referred to as the pure minor scale and as the aeolian mode, and it is the same as the descending melodic minor scale.

The harmonic minor is rather straightforward in that it features a lowered 3rd and 6th; however, the melodic minor scale is unique in that it descends differently than it ascends. The ascending melodic minor scale (jazz minor) is the same as a major scale with a lowered 3rd, while the descending melodic minor scale is the same as the natural minor.

Ex. 2 shows the notes of the *A♭* jazz minor scale as related to *G7.* Remember for this kind of substitution, use the jazz minor scale whose root is *one half-step above* the root of the dominant chord you want to play over.

Next month, we'll work on applying the jazz minor scale and take a look at a few of its fingerings. Until next month, keep practicing, and remember—straight ahead.

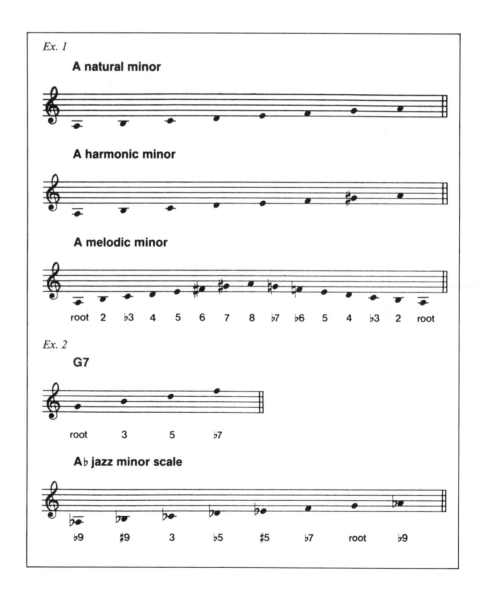

Arnie Berle's
FRETBOARD BASICS

Jazz Minor Fingerings

THE JAZZ MINOR (MELODIC MINOR) SCALE CAN produce some of the most common sounds in contemporary improvisation, as we discussed. Now let's begin to integrate fingerings for this useful tonal sequence into your fretboard arsenal.

You can easily remember the jazz minor's structure if you recall that it is the same as the major scale but with a lowered 3rd. (Below is the *A* jazz minor scale which has a lowered 3rd, *C.*)

The following *G* jazz minor scale has a lowered 3rd, *Bb*.

Here are several moveable fingerings for the jazz minor scale. Be sure to practice them in all positions:

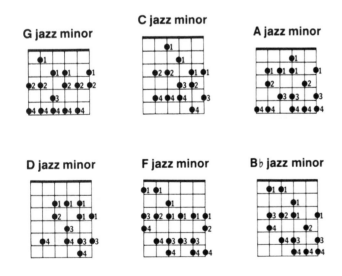

Last month we explored how to superimpose the jazz minor scale over a dominant chord whose root is one half-step lower than the root of the scale. (For example, for *G7,* use the *Ab* jazz minor scale.) Now let's look at a few lines, which will help you hear how this type of substitution sounds in context. The following phrases are based on the II V I chords in the key of *Db (Ebm7, Ab7,* and *Dbmaj7).* Remember that you should use the *A* jazz minor scale for *Ab7*:

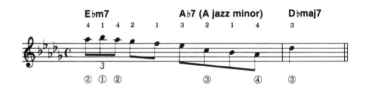

To better understand where the preceding fingerings originate, analyze the *Db* major scale pattern starting with the 4th finger positioned on the fifth string, 4th fret (also analyze the fingering that starts on the sixth string, 9th fret). Practice the two *A* jazz minor fingerings that begin on the sixth string, 5th fret. (One starts with the left-hand pinky, while the other uses the 4th finger.)

This is a lot of material to absorb, so take your time and learn it well. Be sure that you thoroughly learn one fingering before proceeding to the next. Merry Christmas, and until next time, "straight ahead."

74

Arnie Berle's
FRETBOARD BASICS

Connecting Licks

ONE QUESTION READERS FRE-quently ask concerns how to improvise. Spontaneously creating music is not always what it appears to be. Although a musician might occasionally dig deep down into his or her subconscious and play brilliant ideas previously undreamed-of, most solos are not developed out of thin air, but rather assembled through familiar avenues where both the mind and fingers have been many times.

The best jazz players have spent years filling their memory banks with improvisational material—including scales, arpeggios, patterns, and licks— that they can reshape and reassemble into an infinite number of variations, depending on what's called for. But how does one accumulate this information? In the same way that a person develops a large spoken vocabulary—through memorization and knowing how to expand a fragment into a number of variations. You can learn how to build your arsenal of licks using several sources, including lessons, records (transcribing solos), and the many books currently available.

Once you've memorized a lick, you must know how and when to use it. So that you can mentally organize licks according to function, you have to be aware of their *chord quality*—whether they're major, minor, or dominant—which can be ascertained through analysis. The ideas in Ex. 1 are grouped according to types of chords they fit. (As you gain experience, you'll begin to realize that some licks have more than one function.) When working from records, always be sure to determine the chord upon which a lick is based. Although most collections of solos conveniently include the chord changes, taking licks off of records is the best way to learn because you can hear nuances such as accents, bends, and slides.

After memorizing a number of licks, you're ready to begin improvising by combining them into phrases that fit common chord progressions. Ex. 2 shows several lines that work for a II V I sequence; notice how the same lick can be used with a number of other ones. I like to hear a smooth flow from one idea to the next, but how elements are as-

sembled varies from player to player. In this month's examples, observe that the licks generally ascend or descend into one an-other by one note. Next month, we'll conclude our discussion of phrase construction. Until then, "straight ahead."

Arnie Berle's
FRETBOARD BASICS

Linking Licks

SINCE MANY BEGINNING STUdents have trouble constructing long, smooth lines out of short memorized licks, let's take a look at some ways to help you produce better solos. (Once you're comfortable with the following material, apply it not only to all keys, but also to all possible fretboard locations.)

A very effective way to expand your improvisational vocabulary is to build phrases from every degree of a given scale (be aware of the various harmonies a particular scale fits). The phrases shown in Ex. 1 fit the *G7* chord; each fragment begins with a different note of the *G* mixolydian mode.

To illustrate the beauty of how being able to play off of any note can dramatically expand your improvisational resources, let's consider a II V progression in the key of *C*. If you play a melodic idea for *Dm7* (II in the key of *C*), regardless of what the last note is, you'll be able to smoothly segue into the *G7* (V) in the next bar. For instance, if the last note of your lick for *Dm7* is *E*, you should be able to start your line for *G7* on either *F* (a scale tone above *E*) or *D* (a scale tone below *E*), depending upon the direction you want to take your concept. Ex. 2 is one example of what you might do in either case.

But don't think that all licks have to be joined as in the preceding example. With experience and practice, you'll learn to connect phrases in almost limitless ways. In Ex. 3, the distance between the last note of the first bar and the first note of the second bar is a minor third.

Last month, I mentioned how jazz players spontaneously reassemble their licks, creating fresh-sounding ideas. An example of how you might vary a melodic idea by modifying its melodic and rhythmic structure is shown in Ex. 4.

Once you can reshape your vocabulary of licks at will, you're on your way to becoming a true improvisor. To help you better understand how improvisations can be constructed, my next few columns will be devoted to analyzing recorded solos, starting with the title cut from an upcoming album by New York-based jazz guitarist Jack Wilkins. Until then, "straight ahead."

Arnie Berle's
FRETBOARD BASICS

April 1986

Playing Around The Melody

SINCE THE BULK OF MY MAIL OVER THE PAST YEAR regarded improvisation, I'd like to devote this month's column to that subject. One of the most common questions readers ask is, "I know all of the scales and arpeggios, but I still can't come up with anything when I try to improvise. What can I do?" Last month, I suggested that you use a familiar melody as a basis for your improvisation, which gives you something to hang onto as you venture out into the deep end, so to speak.

Now let's see how the process works. The examples include several improvisations based on a melody. Notice that the original tune is always lurking within each variation regardless of the complexity.

Upper and lower neighboring notes are used to embellish the melody (see my June '84 column); observe how the original tune is always going in and out of the improvised one. As you develop your skills, you'll eventually be able to go further and further away from the original idea and begin to improvise completely new lines.

Next month, I'll answer more mail. Until then, if anybody asks where you're heading, tell them "straight ahead!"

Arnie Berle's
FRETBOARD BASICS

May 1986

Basic Blues

OVER THE PAST YEAR, A NUMBER OF READERS have asked me to discuss blues and rock scales, so this column is devoted to some common fingerings. One of the main advantages of the blues scale is that it fits a number of chords. Since so much of rock music is based on the blues, the blues scale plays a very important role in pop music.

The basic blues pentatonic scale has five notes ("penta" means five): root, $\flat$3, 4, 5, $\flat$7. Players such as B.B. King frequently add the $\flat$5, creating what is commonly known as the blues scale. The formula for the basic blues scale reads root, $\flat$3, 4, 5, $\flat$7, and in the key of *F*, the notes are *F, A$\flat$, C,* and *E$\flat$*. The following diagram shows the *F* blues scale in the first position. I call this fingering Form 1 because the root, or 1, is the lowest available note.

F blues scale
form 1

The preceding form combined with the following fingerings enable you to play the *F* blues scale over the entire length of the fingerboard (notice that I've named the forms after the lowest available note in each pattern). In Form 4, the 1st finger is placed at the 6th fret (*B$\flat$*). When you get to the third string, reach back to get *C* at the 5th fret: however, keep in mind that you can also start the scale with your 2nd finger, play the next note (*C*) with your 4th finger, and so on, which leaves the first finger free for the *C* on the third string.

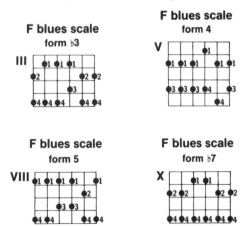

Remember that each scale fingering is moveable and should be practiced up and down the fingerboard (it's very important that you know the name of each scale at every point along the neck). For example, if you want to play a *C* blues scale that covers a relatively low range, you can use Form 5 starting on *G*, sixth string, 3rd fret. The note G is the 5th of the *C* blues scale, which reads *C* (root), *E$\flat$* ($\flat$3), *F* (4), *G* (5), *B$\flat$* ($\flat$7). Here's a diagram of Form 5 in the key of *C*:

C blues scale
form 5

By moving the preceding fingering down two frets, you have the *B$\flat$* blues scale, starting on the note *F*.

Let's explore another example of moveable scale fingerings. If you want to play a low-register *E* blues scale, Form $\flat$3 works nicely. Observe that the lowest available note of the following fingering is *G*, the $\flat$3 of the key of *E* major. The notes of the *E* blues scale are *E* (root), *G* ($\flat$3), *A* (4), *B* (5), *D* ($\flat$7).

E blues scale
form $\flat$3

It's very important to be able to smoothly move from one fingering to another; each pattern facilitates its own assortment of licks. The next diagram shows a common pattern that moves from Form 1 up to Form $\flat$3. By combining both scale fingerings, you now have a much wider range of notes for your improvisation.

This should give you plenty of material to practice until next month, when we'll see how the blues scale is related to other pentatonic scales. Until then, "straight ahead."

78

Arnie Berle's
FRETBOARD BASICS

June 1986

More Blues Basics

BEFORE WE GET THIS COLUMN UNDER WAY, LET'S RE-view the material covered last month, where I presented diagrams for the basic blues scale that cover the entire fingerboard. The basic blues scale includes the root, $\flat$3, 4, 5, and $\flat$7; here it is in the key of F:

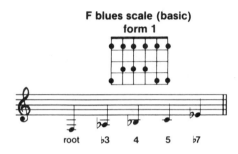

F blues scale (basic)
form 1

root $\flat$3 4 5 $\flat$7

Another form of the blues scale preferred by many players includes the $\flat$5 ($\sharp$4) of the major scale; the formula for this version is root, $\flat$3, 4, $\sharp$4 ($\flat$5), 5, $\flat$7. *[Ed. Note: Some players refer to the five-note blues scale as the "blues pentatonic scale" ("penta" means five) and the six-note version as the "blues scale."]*

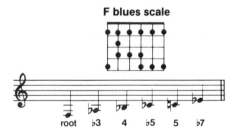

F blues scale

root $\flat$3 4 $\flat$5 5 $\flat$7

Many rock guitarists prefer the basic form of the blues scale because it can be used in situations other than the blues. The following example has the same notes as the basic F blues scale; however, this starts on $A\flat$. In relation to the key of $A\flat$, this new scale is called the $A\flat$ pentatonic scale and reads root, 2, 3, 5, 6:

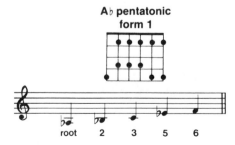

A$\flat$ pentatonic
form 1

root 2 3 5 6

Here's the new pentatonic scale in three keys. Notice the similarities between the $B\flat$ pentatonic scale shown below, and the G blues scale:

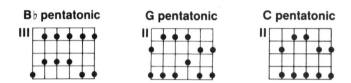

B$\flat$ pentatonic   **G pentatonic**   **C pentatonic**

These diagrams illustrate two extended versions of the pentatonic scale, giving you a wider range of notes to choose from:

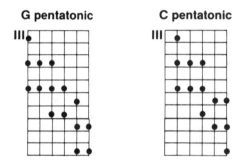

G pentatonic   **C pentatonic**

Again, the notes of the basic F blues scale are the same as the $A\flat$ pentatonic scale. Although both scales contain the same notes, it's important that you understand how to use them separately. The blues scale can be played over the dominant 7th chord, the minor 7th chord, and the I, IV, and V chords of the common 12-bar blues progression. In the key of F, you can use the basic F blues scale for $F7$, $Fm7$, and the F 12-bar blues progression with $F7$, $B\flat7$, and $C7$.

On the other hand, the pentatonic scale fits major-type chords such as $A\flat$ and $A\flat6$. If the two scales share the same elements, why aren't they interchangeable? The situation is similar to how the C major scale has exactly the same notes as the G mixolydian mode. Although they contain the same components, the more you learn to think of them independently, the more you'll be able to play within the sound of the chord at hand, and the less you'll get confused.

Now compare the differences in *sound* between the basic G blues scale and the G pentatonic scale. The basic blues scale has a lowered 3rd, giving it a blues flavor, while the pentatonic scale has a regular 3rd, giving it a major flavor.

Since they have notes in common, the basic blues scale and the pentatonic scale can be thought of in terms of various relationships. For instance, if you're playing a G blues scale, you are also playing the $B\flat$ pentatonic scale, a minor third higher than G. Similarly, if you're playing a C blues, you can think in terms of the $E\flat$ pentatonic scale. Next month, we'll tackle a new series. Until then, "straight ahead."

Arnie Berle's
FRETBOARD BASICS

Vertical Scales

PLAYING SCALES HORIZONTALLY ALONG EACH STRING can be challenging, as well as beneficial (as you saw last month, when we explored all 12 major keys). Horizontal movement requires having to shift your hand position up or down the string.

Now let's examine playing major scales while keeping your left hand stationary in one position, eliminating the need to shift all over the fingerboard. This technique is called *position playing,* and it necessitates executing all of the notes in a four-fret fingerboard area. For example, to play in the second position, orient your left-hand 1st finger to the 2nd fret; your remaining three fingers fall into place at frets three, four, and five, respectively (stretching down with the 1st finger or up with the 4th does not constitute a position change).

Here are diagrams of the four basic scales in second position. Each fingering is labeled according to its form, which helps to identify it when moved to another position. Notice that the lower and upper tonic notes of each scale are indicated by circles; notes above or below the tonics are also in the same key. The Form 3 scale has an alternate fingering for the G# on the second line of the staff (from the bottom); the context of a particular phrase determines the fingering you should use.

G Scale Form 1   **C Scale Form 2**

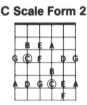

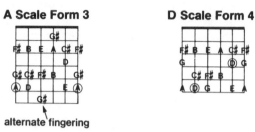

alternate fingering

This Form 5 fingering requires left-hand stretching ability, and has practical application:

F Scale Form 5

Ex. 1 shows the notation for the first four diagrams (the strings are indicated through the diagrams). It's important to remember that you can play in five different keys in any fretboard position. For example, in the third position, you can play in A♭ (with Form 1 fingering), D♭ (Form 2), B♭ (Form 3), E♭ (Form 4), and G (Form 5). Make a point of learning the five keys for each position. Also, select a piece of music and read it in different positions. Be sure to place your hand in the correct fingerboard location.

Next month we'll see how to connect some of the forms. Until then, "straight ahead."

Ex. 1
G Scale Form 1

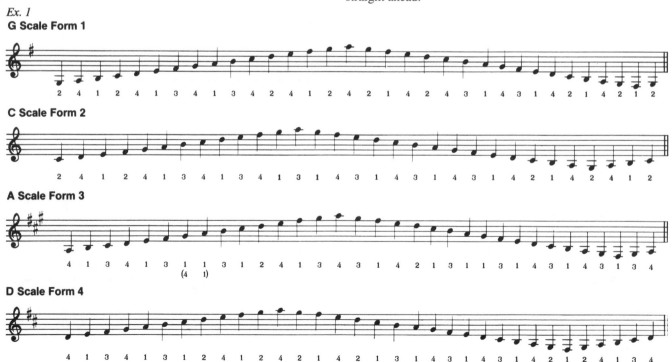

Arnie Berle's
FRETBOARD BASICS

Position Playing

USING FIVE DIFFERENT FINGERINGS, YOU can play in five different keys without changing your position on the fretboard. For example, by keeping your hand in the second position, you can play in the keys of *C, G, D, A,* and *F* (this approach was covered in my Feb. '87 column).

Of course, sometimes it is more practical to switch positions in the same key. Reasons for changing positions include (1) the inherent tonal quality of each fingering, (2) to the make fingering more convenient, and (3) to expand the range of a passage. Now let's investigate changing positions in the key of *C.*

Ex. 1 features a *C* scale starting with the Form 2 fingering (again, see my Feb. '87 column). Notice how you switch to the Form 3 fingering, which leads to another part of the fingerboard. The switch from Form 2 to Form 3 is made on the third string and is a half-step shift. Changing from Form 3 to Form 1 is not uncommon; see Ex. 2. Observe that the Form 3 fingering uses the alternate note on the fourth string, which is the shifting point into the Form 1 fingering.

In Ex. 3, you change from Form 1 to Form 5; the switch is made on the fifth string and involves a half-step shift. Ex. 4 shows the Form 5 scale fingering switching to Form 4. Here the change is made on the third string.

All position changes should be practiced all over the fingerboard and in all keys. In an actual playing situation, chances are that you will never have to play through all the forms in any one key. In most situations, you start in one key and then move through a number of different ones before returning to the original. Just looking at a tune's key signature can be very deceiving. For example, the standard "Laura" is in *C* major (with no sharps or flats), but if you look at the chords, you'll notice that the first four bars are based on the key of *G.* The next four bars are in *F,* and the following four are in *E♭.* So it's important to examine a song's chords, which reveal the keys you will be playing in.

Ex. 5 starts out in *C* major; begin by using Form 2. The second measure has accidentals in it that suggest the keys of *A♭* and *E♭.* For study purposes, let's consider the key of *E♭.* Prepare to play in *E♭,* using Form 4 in third position. In bar 3 there are more accidentals, suggesting the key of *A;* here use Form 1 in the fourth position. In the last measure, you return to *C,* with Form 3 in the fifth position. Ex. 6 demonstrates how music moves through different keys; observe the possible scale fingerings.

The preceding examples could have been fingered any number of ways. Remember: There is more than one way to play most things on the guitar. Most good guitarists ask themselves these two questions: (1) Where does a passage sound best and (2) where is the easiest place to play it?

Next month we'll look at how Jay Berliner, one of America's leading studio guitarists, approaches fingering difficult passages. Until then, straight ahead.

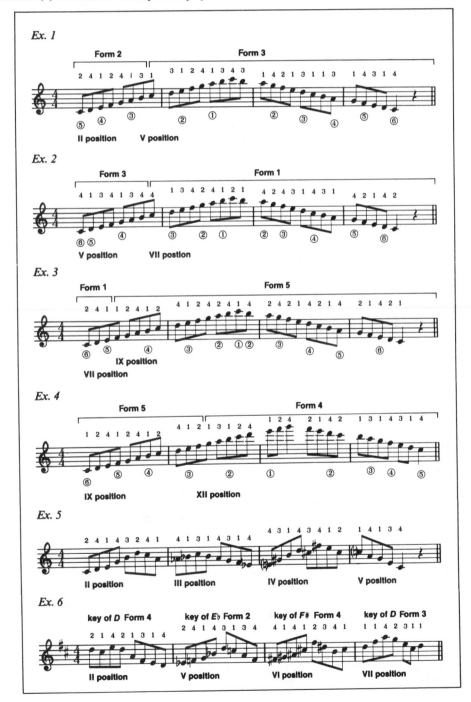

Arnie Berle's
FRETBOARD BASICS

Reading Rhythms

READING MUSIC IS MORE THAN JUST BEING ABLE TO find the notes on your guitar; it also means being able to play things in the correct rhythm. In the March '87 issue of *Guitar Player* Jeff Berlin presented many good reasons to learn to read music. I was reminded of a couple of his points recently, as I observed a recording session for a wine commercial. While the guitarist, Craig Snyder, was required to read only chord charts, the notated rhythms were tricky. In the lucrative field of session work, reading is often a necessary skill, so keep in mind that the pains you take to become a better reader will eventually pay off.

Still another reason to improve your reading is to expand your musical horizons. Many books are available that contain transcribed solos by top instrumentalists. In addition, a lot of *Guitar Player's* music is written in standard notation. To learn anything correctly, it's usually best to go back to the basics; for those of you who can handle rhythmic notation already, use this column as a review.

If you want to draw a line that is as straight as possible, you should use a ruler, and if you want to accurately measure off three minutes, you should use a clock. In music it's also important to have some means of measuring various note values in a piece of music. In a recording studio, musicians frequently wear headphones so they can hear a click track. However, most of you don't have that luxury when practicing at home, so you'll have to rely on a metronome or your foot.

Steadily tapping your foot helps you to interpret the note values with a high degree of accuracy. For example, when you see a whole-note (o), tap your foot evenly four times. A half-note (♩) gets two taps, while a quarter-note (♩) gets one tap. A dot after a note increases the value of the note by half; therefore, a dotted half-note (♩.) gets three taps. The following exercises will help you get used to tapping and playing at the same time. I've kept them simple so that they won't get in the way of tapping your foot.

Before you tackle the following exercises, keep in mind that counting out loud is another very helpful way to keep the time accurate and to know where you are in the measure. (The numbers beneath each note are what should be spoken.) This first exercise features quarter-notes; observe that the fourth beat in the last measure is a quarter-rest, which means that you don't play for one count (but you still tap your foot). Here goes:

The next example is based on half-notes. The symbol in bars 2 and 4 is a half-rest (don't play for two beats, but be sure to tap):

Now play the next exercise, based on dotted half-notes. Notice that bars 4 and 8 each contain three counts of rest. Remember to keep tapping and counting through the rests:

Here is an exercise based on whole-notes, with whole-rests in bars 4 and 8. Remember that these simple exercises are intended to help you get used to tapping as you play:

Finally, these examples are based on combinations of the note values used previously. Keep a steady, even beat with your foot throughout each exercise. Don't rush the counts, and don't rush through the rests. Give every note and rest its full value.

The best thing you can do for yourself now is what all good studio musicians have always done to keep their reading skills sharp—pick up some good beginning clarinet, flute, or saxophone books, and just read through the first several pages. In their first few pages, most beginning books don't go beyond the rhythms you've just learned. Keep tapping your foot, and you won't have any problem with more complex rhythms.

Next month I'll introduce eighth-notes and sixteenths. Until then, "straight ahead."

Arnie Berle's
FRETBOARD BASICS

August 1987

Eighth-Note Rhythms

THE ABILITY TO READ RHYTHMS WELL GOES HAND IN hand with being a good guitarist. Last month I introduced a series of exercises that use quarter-notes, half-notes, whole-notes, dotted notes, and rests. This month, let's take a look at eighth-notes.

A single eighth-note has a flag (♪), while groups of two and four eighth-notes are usually connected with a beam (♫ or ♬). Remember that two eighth-notes are played in one beat, count, or foot tap, and they should be played evenly. The following example shows a series of eighth-notes; play one note when your foot goes down, and then play the next one when your foot goes up. Count aloud, saying the number of the beat on the downbeat (when your foot goes down) and "and" on the upbeat (when your foot goes up). The arrows indicate the direction of your foot taps:

Now play this exercise, which combines eighth-notes with last month's rhythms. Only one pitch is used so that you can concentrate on the rhythmic scheme:

These drills feature a rhythmic mix and a variety of notes:

Every note has a corresponding rest. The eighth-note rest (⁷) lasts for half of a beat and can be found on either the downbeat or the upbeat:

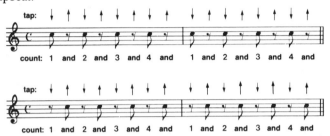

Here are various combinations of note values in context with eighth-note rests. Count out loud, tap your foot, and don't rush the upbeat, which is a common problem with beginning readers:

It really helps to sing an unfamiliar rhythm before you play it. This can be done by singing a syllable such as "da" or "la." Once you can sing a rhythm well, you'll find that it's much easier to play. Here is sample of a rhythm that might be sung. Don't forget to tap your foot while singing.

None of these exercises will be useful to you unless you expand your efforts by working with other material. Clarinet, sax, and flute books are excellent sources of single-note exercises and melodies. You can only become a good reader by reading. Until next month, "straight ahead."

Arnie Berle's
FRETBOARD BASICS

September 1987

Reading Ties

ONE OF THE MOST COMMON WAYS TO EXTEND THE TIME value of a note is to use a tie—a curved line that joins two or more notes of the *same pitch*—so it's essential that you practice music that includes them. This month, let's tackle some examples that combine ties with the notes, rests, and rhythms from my last few columns.

The following examples show notes that are tied over the bar line. In each case, play the first note of the tied group, holding it for its own time value *plus* the duration of the note it's connected to. Here the tied notes occur on the fourth beat (or count). Don't forget to tap your foot and count out loud:

In this example, don't pick the first eighth-note in each measure. Instead think of it as being part of the note it immediately follows. After each tie, the next note is played on the "and" of the third beat:

Don't forget that there are other ways to increase a note's time value. *A dot* placed after a note increases the duration of that note by half. My July '87 column discussed how a dotted half-note is worth three quarter-note beats, which is the same as using a tie to join a half-note to a quarter-note (of the same pitch):

In many cases, a dot can be used instead of a tie. Although the following examples are notated differently, they sound and are played the same.

These two examples *look* different, but they are played the same. (A dotted quarter-note is a beat-and-a-half long.)

Here are more phrases illustrating how dots can replace some ties. When you play the music, be sure to tap your foot and count:

Finally, tackle these long examples:

Keep in mind that many studio musicians keep their skills sharp by reading through clarinet, flute, or trumpet books. Remember: If you don't practice sight-reading, you won't improve. Next month we'll cover sixteenth-notes. Until then, "straight ahead!"

The author of numerous instruction books, Arnie Berle teaches at Mercy College in Dobbs Ferry, New York, and at his studio in Yonkers, New York.

Arnie Berle's
FRETBOARD BASICS

Sight-Reading Sixteenths

BEFORE WE MOVE ON TO A NEW AREA OF SIGHT-READing, I want to again stress the importance of tapping your foot. When you keep time by tapping, you establish the basic pulse to which you can relate all of a piece's different note values.

At the beginning of each piece is what appears to be a fraction—the time signature. When the lower of the two numbers is a 4, as in 6/4, 5/4, 4/4, 3/4, or 2/4, it means that the quarter-note gets the beat (a half-note gets two beats, etc.), or foot tap. Observe that your foot's tapping action has two parts: (1) the down movement, representing the downbeat, and (2) the up movement, or the upbeat. In my Aug. '87 column you learned that you can play one note on the downbeat and another note on the upbeat; these are called eighth-notes. Two eighth-notes are equal to one quarter-note. To go a step further, keep in mind that you can play two notes in either the downbeat or the upbeat portion of the eighth note. These notes, which are exactly half as long as an eighth, are called sixteenth-notes. Two sixteenth-notes look like this (♫), and are equal to one eighth (♪). Here is an exercise that shows an eighth-note on the downbeat and two sixteenths on the upbeat. Tap slowly and evenly:

The following exercise shows two sixteenth-notes played on the downbeat, and one eighth-note played on the upbeat:

Here are four consecutive sixteenth-notes; each grouping equals one quarter-note:

Now let's combine the preceding sixteenth-note rhythms. Before you tackle these examples, try singing "da" or "la" to each note:

Last month you learned that placing a dot after a note increases the value of that note by one-half; therefore, a dotted eighth is equal to an eighth plus a sixteenth, or three sixteenths. A dotted eighth-note is usually followed by a sixteenth-note. While a tie can be used to notate the long/short sound of a dotted eighth followed by a sixteenth, writing the figure with a dot has fewer elements and is easier to read:

Finally, tackle these exercises. Tap your foot slowly and evenly and singing the rhythms before you play the music:

If you want to be a good sight-reader, it's essential that you practice regularly. To increase your understanding of different note values, you have to keep reading. Next month we'll cover the triplet. Until then, straight ahead!

Arnie Berle's
FRETBOARD BASICS

November 1987

Reading Triplets

ONE OF THE BEST WAYS TO DEVELOP your sight-reading skills is to work with a wide variety of music. In addition, practicing all kinds of scales and arpeggios helps you to cultivate strong technique. This month let's concentrate on reading triplet-based rhythms.

> **Cultivate Strong Technique By Practicing All Kinds Of Scales & Arpeggios**

The triplet divides the beat into three equal parts. The basic triplet looks like this (♪♪♪), and it is played in the space of one quarter-note (♩). Ex. 1 alternates measures of quarter-notes and triplets. Observe how the word "triplet" is divided into syllables that correspond to each part of the figure.

Ex. 2 shows an alternate way of counting the triplet that keeps track of the beat. Ex. 3 uses triplets only. If you can execute the triplets evenly, feel free to stop saying the syllables as you play. Several rather short jazz-type licks that include triplets are shown in Ex. 4. The phrases in Ex. 5 are longer. The ties make things trickier.

So far, we've dealt only with eighth-note triplets. The *quarter-note* triplet looks like this (♩♩♩), and it is played in the space of two quarter-notes. This is a tricky figure to play; Ex. 5 shows how it can be subdivided.

When you practice sight-reading, make sure that your material includes a wide variety of rhythmic figures. Next month we'll talk about syncopation. Until then, "straight ahead."

The author of numerous instruction books, Arnie Berle teaches at Mercy College in Dobbs Ferry, New York, and at his studio in Yonkers, New York.

86

Arnie Berle's
FRETBOARD BASICS

Handling Syncopated Rhythms

GOOD SIGHT-READING INVOLVES MORE than just being able to name the notes on the page—you also must be able to play the correct notes in the correct time with the proper expression. Since July '87, this column has been devoted to learning a wide range of notes and rests. This month let's talk about syncopated rhythmic figures.

Syncopation refers to accents that are placed where you least expect them. In a bar of 4/4, there is a natural tendency to accent the first and third beats, which are the strong points of a measure. In syncopated music, however, the weak second and fourth beats are accented, as well as notes that are off of the beat.

One of the most commonly used syncopated patterns employs three notes: an eighth, a quarter, and an eighth, in that order. This pattern is very common, and it appears in many variations, so it's important for you to fully understand how to count it. One of the trickiest parts of the pattern—and of all syncopated figures—is that the downbeats are harder to see, which makes sight-reading more difficult. Ex. 1 shows how to count this syncopation and how it relates to straight eighth-notes.

Notice how the tied eighths can be notated as quarters. When reading the eighth/quarter/eighth pattern, it helps to visualize where the downbeat is in respect to each quarter-note.

The other examples show several variations on the syncopation in Ex. 1. Don't forget to tap your foot steadily and count out loud as you play through each measure; see Ex. 2.

A measure with a lot of rests can be harder to read than one with lots of notes, so you might find it helpful to pencil-in where the beats occur. Practice Ex. 3 until they come automatically.

A common device used by many composers and jazz soloists is the double-time feel, where a line changes from eighths to sixteenths. The phrases in Ex. 4 *sound the* same; however, in the first bar you tap your foot twice, while in the second you tap four times.

Ex. 5 is another example of a sixteenth-note pattern versus an equivalent one written in eighth-notes (by now you should realize that the sixteenth/eighth/sixteenth pattern is the same as four sixteenths with the second and third notes tied together).

Now test your rhythm skills and play Ex. 6, an eight-bar solo that switches to a double time feel in measure 3. Until next month, "straight ahead."

Chord Connections

ONE OF THE BEAUTIES OF THREE-NOTE chords has to do with the smooth ways in which they can be connected. Seamless transitions from one chord to the next in a harmonized scale can be achieved by using passing diminished 7th chords, which can spice up a bland, static progression.

The diminished 7th chord is one of the most common passing harmonies. Keep in mind that a passing chord connects two closely related chords. Ex. 1 is an *F* harmonized scale with diminished 7th passing chords. Ex. 2 shows a harmonized

scale with passing diminished 7th chords that move across the fretboard. I highly recommend practicing all harmonized scales with diminished 7th passing chords in this same manner.

Ex. 3 shows what might be done when you have a I (tonic) chord for a whole measure. Observe the *Am7* chord on the fourth beat, which is nothing more than an *Fmaj9* chord with some notes omitted; in this case, IIIm7 substitutes for I. In Ex. 4, the diminished 7th is used as a substitute for VIm7 in the very common I-VIm7-IIm7-V7 pro-

gression. Notice that this three-note D7 omits the root.

Finally, Ex. 5 and Ex. 6 show how to connect a series of dominant 7th chords. To retain the sound of the progression, keep the appropriate dominant 7th chord on the first beat of each measure, and then proceed up or down the harmonized scale (don't forget that in Ex. 5, *C7* is the V of *Fmaj7, G7* is the V of *C7*, and *D7* is the V of *G7*.)

Arnie Berle's
FRETBOARD BASICS

December 1989

9th Chord Voicings

WE'VE BEEN WORKING WITH 7TH CHORDS FOR SEVeral months. Now let's expand our vocabulary by extending the chords we've learned.

Ex. 1 shows the 7th chords that occur diatonically within the major scale. Each is formed by adding notes in thirds above the root. In the *Cmaj7,* for example, an *E* is placed above the *C, G* above *E,* and *B* above *G.* To extend each chord, simply add an additional note a third above. The chords shown in Ex. 2a are called 9ths because the new note is a ninth above the root. If we add another third, we derive the 11th chords in Ex. 2b, and yet another third yields the 13th chords in Ex. 2c. (Remember, the Roman numerals indicate the position of the chord within the scale.)

The farther we extend the chords, the more difficult it is to play the complete voicings on the guitar. Usually, some notes are omitted. A few commonly used extended chords are shown in Ex. 3. Notice that when a chord is extended, it is usually best to support the added notes by retaining the 7th. And when the 11th is added to a major chord, it is usually raised, as in the *Cmaj9#11* shown.

The chords in Ex. 4 are extensions of the minor 7th chord. Ex. 5 shows extensions of the dominant 7th chord. Again, the 11th is usually raised. Ex. 6 shows two extended-chord versions of the II-V-I progression. Notice how the voices move smoothly from one chord to the next.

Try creating extended chord forms on your own. You can often get a good-sounding 9th chord by moving the root up two frets, and raising the 5th of a dominant chord yields a 13th chord.

Next month we'll explore altered chords. Till then, "straight ahead."

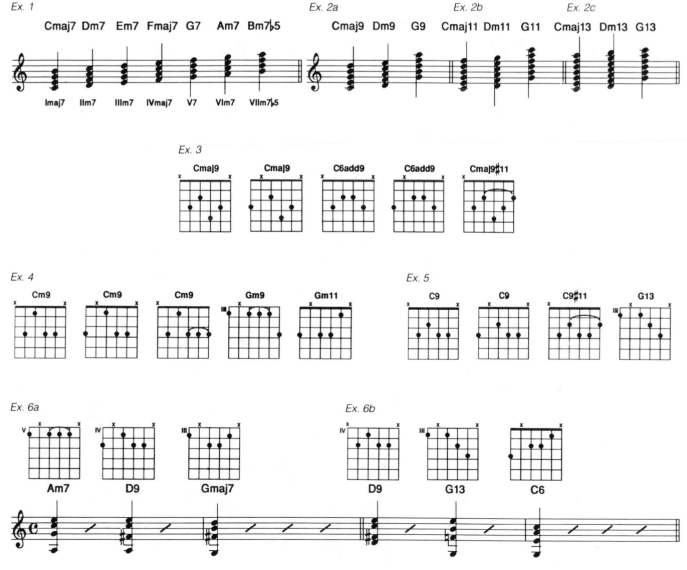

89

Arnie Berle's
FRETBOARD BASICS

January 1990

Introducing Altered Chords

ALTERED CHORDS CONTAIN ONE OR MORE NOTES NOT in the original scale or key from which they're derived. The most commonly altered notes are the 5th and the 9th, both of which may be raised or lowered a half-step. Altered chords can create a more interesting, colorful progression when accompanying a singer or an instrumental solo. The progressions shown here should be transposed to other keys and played all over the fingerboard.

Ex. 1 is based on a II-V-I progression in *G*. Note how the *D7♭5* with the ♭5 in the bass creates a chromatically descending bass line that leads to the root of the *Gmaj7* chord. The *Gmaj7-G6* progression gives another melodic line, this time on the fourth string.

In Ex. 2, notice how E, the 9th of the *Dm9* chord, descends to *D♯*, which is the raised 5th of *G7♯5,* then to *D♮*, the 9th of the *Cmaj9* chord. A similar chromatically descending line appears on the second string in Ex. 3.

Notice that the *D7♭5♭9* chord in Ex. 4 is exactly the same as an *A♭7*. The ♭II (in this case, *A♭7*) is a common substitute for *V7* (*D7*).

Ex. 5 features both a raised 9th and a lowered 9th, while Ex. 6 features yet another chromatically descending line—this time on both the first *and* second string. Note how the *D7♭9♯11* fills out the first string chromatic line in Ex. 7. The final example is based on a I-VI-II-V progression, but the VI is dominant, as opposed to the more "normal" m7. Listen to the interesting melodic line in the top voice.

Remember, good guitar accompaniment requires that you move from chord to chord as smoothly as possible. Each note in a chord should move to a note in the following chord without any undue large skips. When two chords have a common tone, that note should be kept. Try to create moving lines like those shown here; we'll have more on moving lines next month. Till then, "straight ahead."

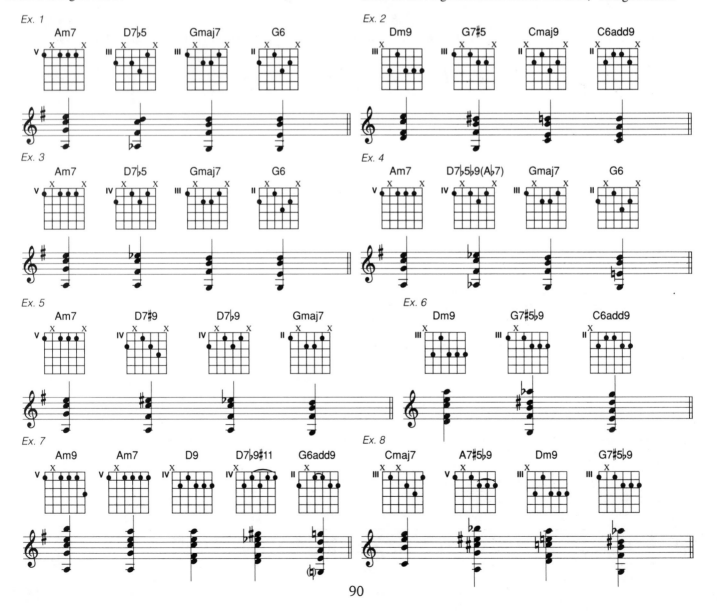

90

Arnie Berle's
FRETBOARD BASICS

Chromatic Movement Within Chords

WE SAW LAST MONTH HOW TO USE ALTERED AND EX-tended chords to create moving melodic lines to connect a series of chords, making a rather bland progression more colorful-sounding and imparting a sense of forward motion. Now let's look at a line commonly implied in minor chord progressions (you'll find it in the first bars of "My Funny Valentine" and "What Are You Doing The Rest Of Your Life" and in the bridge sections of "More" and "Michelle").

In Ex. 1, the moving line occurs on the fourth string. It descends from the root through the major 7th and the minor 7th down to the 6th. (Sometimes the minor/major 7th chord is omitted or given as an augmented chord—*Daug* instead of *Gm maj7* for example.)

Ex. 2 shows another voicing of the progression with the moving line in the bass voice. In Ex. 3, it occurs on the third string. In Ex. 4, the line is in the bass once more, but now on the sixth string (note the alternate fingering for the *Am6* chord). Remember, an *Am6* chord is the same as *D9* without the root. You might, for example, use Ex. 4 as a substitution for an *Am7-D9* progression.

Another three-note voicing is shown in Ex. 5. Here, the descending line appears in the top voice. In Ex. 6, the progression is reversed; the *ascending* line occurs on the fourth string. This pattern can be used any time you have a minor chord that lasts for a measure or more.

I can't adequately stress the importance of thinking in terms of moving lines. They add so much to your accompaniments! Herb Ellis once told me that he always thinks of little melodies when backing someone. That's what separates giants like Herb from the little people. Till next month, "straight ahead."

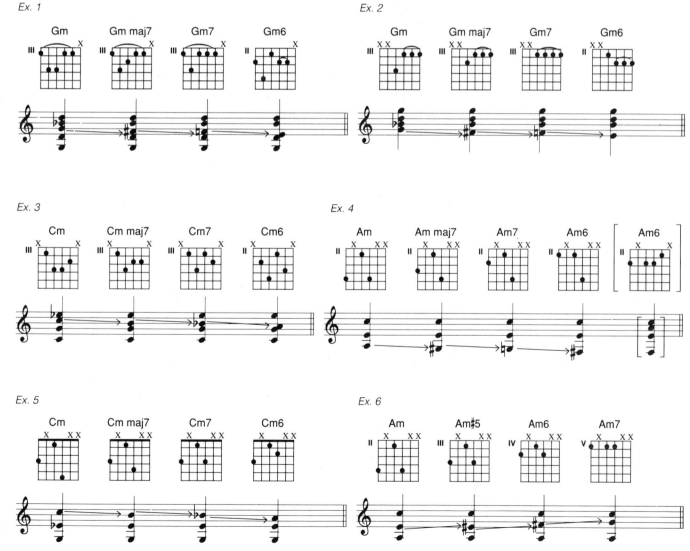

Arnie Berle's
FRETBOARD BASICS

March 1990

An Introduction To Chord-Melody Playing

FOR THE PAST FEW MONTHS WE'VE been looking at extended and altered chords. We've seen how we can use such chords to spice up a bland progression. Now let's move on to the chord-melody style, the technique of creating both chords and melody at the same time. This is one of the most challenging—and pleasurable—ways of playing the guitar.

When playing chord-melody style, it's important to remember three things: The melody is almost always placed in the highest voice of the chord; the melody note tends to appear on the top two strings, and sometimes on the third; and the melody is usually played an octave higher than written. (Getting the melody onto the upper strings by raising the pitch an octave leaves the lower strings free to form the supporting chord.)

We've learned how to play multiple forms of chords so that we could place the root, 3rd, 5th, or 7th in the bass. But for chord melody playing, we need to be able to make the same type of chord with either the root, 3rd, 5th, or 7th in the *top* voice, since that's where the melody tends to be.

How would we go about harmonizing a simple melody like that in Ex. 1? First, raise the pitch an octave. Next, you must decide whether to harmonize every note with its own chord, or only some of the notes. To harmonize each note, we need four types of C7 chord—one with each of the four melody notes in the top voice—and an F chord with an F note on top. Ex. 2 shows one possible harmonization. Note that the third chord is a C9, since the melody note, D, is the 9th of C.

One of the most fun things about chord melody playing is the possibility of reharmonizing a tune. Ex. 3 shows another treatment of our little melody. The G note is harmonized by a Gm7 chord, the 117 chord that precedes C7. (This time, the C note is not harmonized; it's just a passing note between Gm7 and C9.) Since the E note is harmonized by the 7th of G♭7, we now refer to it as F♭. (G♭7 is a half-step approach chord to Fmaj7—see my Nov. '89 column.) The G♭7 creates a descending bass line, which contrasts nicely with the ascending melody.

Ex. 4, a harmonized G major scale, will help you start thinking of how to form chords with different melody notes on top. Each chord is a version of the I chord in the key of G. In some places, I've shown two different chords below a single melody note, just to demonstrate some possibilities. Transpose Ex. 4 into different keys.

Next month we'll do more on chord melody. Till then, "straight ahead."

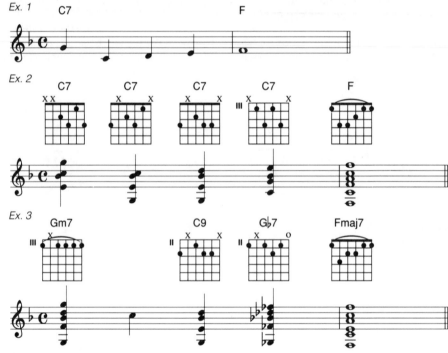

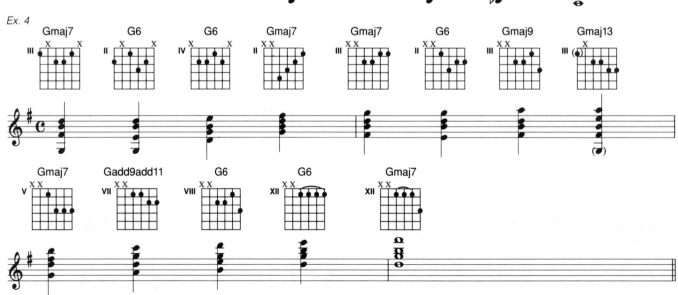

Arnie Berle's
FRETBOARD BASICS

Minors And Dominants In Chord-Melody Playing

WE HAVE BEGUN TO STUDY CHORD-melody playing, a style that allows the guitarist to play melody and chords simultaneously. Since a given melody note is either one of the notes of the prevailing chord or a melodic extension of the chord, it's important to be able to play major, minor, and dominant chords with either the root, 3rd, 5th, 6th, 7th, 9th, 11th, or 13th on top. We saw how to do this with major chords last month; now let's look at minor and dominant chords.

Ex. 1 shows how to place each note of the diatonic scale in the top voice of an *Am7* chord, and Ex. 2 does the same with *D7*.

(You can think of *Am7* and *D7* as II and V in the key of *G*.)

To harmonize a melody note that does not occur diatonically in the scale that generates the chord, simply use the chord form that has as its top voice the note nearest the chromatic tone, and then replace the diatonic note with the chromatic one. For example, you might use one of the first two chords in Ex. 3 to play an *A♯* over a *D7* chord, or use the third chord to play an *E♭*, over *D7*. Notice that the new chord symbols reflect the chromatic tones. The chords are now referred to as altered chords.

Ex. 4 is designed to give you practice in harmonizing chromatic melody notes. The notes are written as they might normally appear in sheet music, but don't forget to raise each one an octave. Next month I'll give you the correct chord forms—be sure to check it out. Till then, "straight ahead."

The author of numerous instruction books, Arnie Berle teaches at Mercy College in Dobbs Ferry, New York, and at his studio in Yonkers, New York.

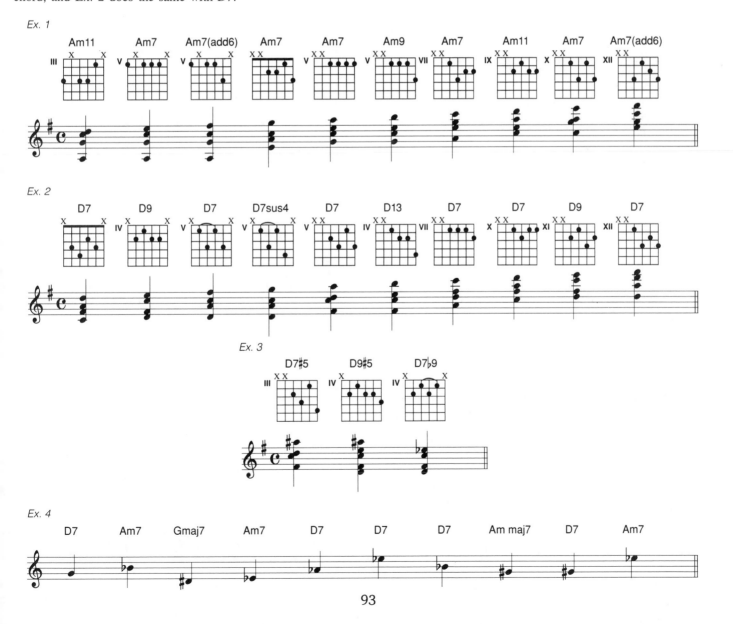

Arnie Berle's
FRETBOARD BASICS

May 1990

Continuing With Chord-Melody Playing

PLAYING CHORD-MELODY STYLE requires that you know a great variety of chord forms so that you can place any possible melody note on the upper strings. With that goal in mind, we've learned how to play major, minor, and dominant chord forms, using the II, V, and I chords in the key of *G* major as our models. Last month we looked at how to deal with melody notes that don't occur diatonically within the key of the piece, and I left you with a short chromatic note quiz. Ex. 1 shows one set of answers, but remember that there are many possible ways to approach each harmony. The chord symbols have been renamed to take into account the new melody notes—the *D7* with a *G* melody note for example, becomes *D7sus4* or *D11*.

Now let's apply what we've learned to a familiar folk melody, "Aura Lee." Ex. 2 shows the first eight bars—since the last four bars are the same as the first four, we'll want to harmonize them differently to create some interest. The harmonization in Ex. 3 uses many of the devices we've recently studied, such as extended and altered chords, substitute chords, and half-step approach chords. Some examples: The *Bm7* in bar 1 substitutes for the original *G*; the *Bb13* in the same

bar is a half-step approach chord to the *A7* in bar 2, which is, in turn, a substitute for the original *Am*; and the *Ab7* in bar 3 is an approach chord to *Gadd9*. Also, note the cycle-of-fourths movement in bars 5 and 6.

Next month we'll look at the remaining eight bars of the tune. Till then, "straight ahead."

The author of numerous instruction books, Arnie Berle teaches at Mercy College in Dobbs Ferry, New York, and at his studio in Yonkers, New York.

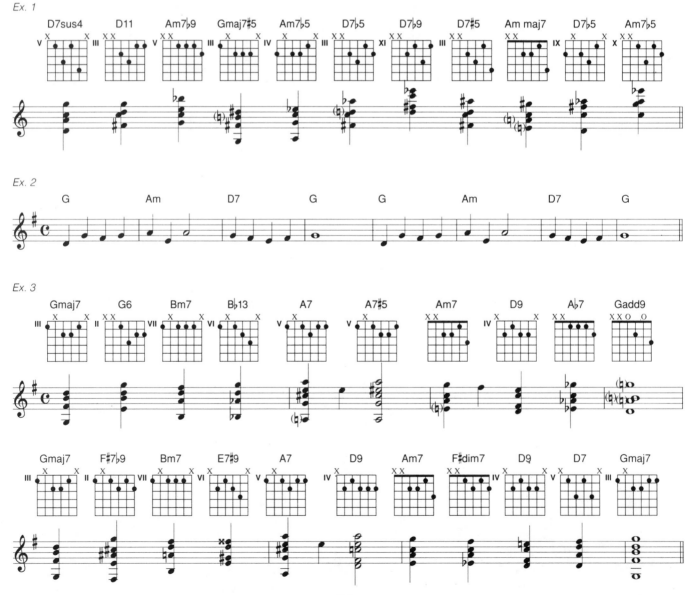

Arnie Berle's
FRETBOARD BASICS

June 1990

Completing Our First Chord-Melody Solo

LET'S LOOK AT THE FINAL EIGHT measures of "Aura Lee" and complete the chord melody solo we started last month. The original melody is shown in Ex. 1. I've included both the original chord progression and a more interesting substitute progression. I've moved the *G7* in bar 2 back two beats and added a *Dm7* to create a II7-V7 progression. This lets us cycle back and put an *A7* chord on the third beat of the first measure. I've preceded the *Gmaj7* in bar 4 with another II7-V7, and I've added *two* II7-V7 progressions in bars 6 and 7.

Now that we've filled out the harmony a bit, we can take it a step further by adding some more colorful substitutions and half-step approach chords, as shown in Ex. 2. The *Em7* in bar 1 is a VI chord substitute for I, while the *Eb7#5 is* a half-step approach chord to the *Dm7add6* in bar 2. (You can also think of the *Eb7#5* as a tritone substitution for the original *A7.*) Notice the additional half-step approach chords in bars 2, 3, 5, and 7.

When a melody note is altered in relation to the prevailing chord, you must indicate the altered note in the chord symbol, as with the *Ab7b9* in the third measure.

I've substantially reharmonized "Aura Lee"

in order to show the possibilities that are available. But in many cases the best setting for a simple tune is the simple, original harmonization.

The author of numerous instruction books, Arnie Berle teaches at Mercy College in Dobbs Ferry, New York, and at his studio in Yonkers, New York.

Aura Lee

Traditional

Ex. 1

original chords:	G	G7	C	G	G B7 E7	Am	D7	G
substitute progression:	Gmaj7 A7	Dm7 G7	Cmaj7 Am7 D7	Gmaj7	G6 B7 E7	Am7 D7	Am7 D7	Gmaj7

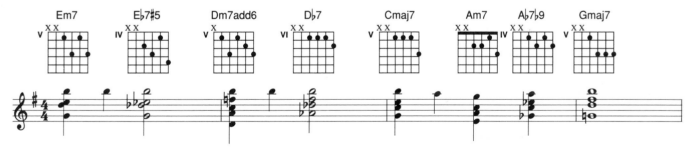

Ex. 2

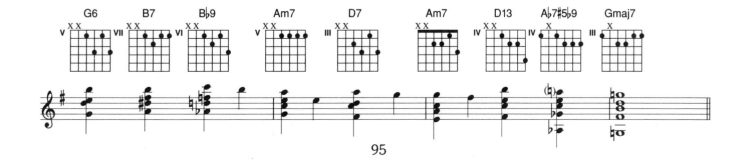

95